Along the Way

By Hilton Kemp

Along the Way

By Hilton Kemp

Text Copyright © 2006 Hilton Kemp.
Cover Design © 2019 Tim Wander and Mark Lloyd.

First Published by Nu-Age Productions,
289 Padiham Road, Burnely, Lancs, BB12 0HA in 2006.

Second Edition
Updated and Reformatted, 2020, by TRW Design and Print.
c/o www.marconibooks.co.uk
First Published by New Generation Publishing in 2020.

The author asserts his moral right under the Copyright, Designs and Patents Act 1988 to be identified as the authors of this work.

A CIP catalogue record for this book is available from the British Library.

ISBN 978-1-80031-951-6

www.newgeneration-publishing.com

New Generation Publishing

*This book is dedicated to my family
and all who may be interested enough to read it.*

Hilton

Cover Photographs
Main: Calcutta, (1943).
Top: The Wedding (1946).
Middle: Barry, Gwen & Hilton on a motorbike (1949).
Bottom: Aged 96 with war medals (2017).

Preface

This is the life story of an ordinary working class chap. He was born in 1921, during the depression of the 1920s and 1930s, and was given an average education at a church school in the town of Ryde. At the age of 14, the school leaving age at that time, he started work.

His father had succeeded in finding him a job with the local gas company, as an apprentice fitter. During the time of Munich, when Hitler was boasting that he would conquer the world, he joined the Territorial Army Royal Engineers Searchlight Regiment.

He was called up in August 1939 for what was termed one month's enlistment. War was declared on the 3rd September and that month stretched to six years' war service, he eventually ended up in Burma.

After demobilisation he married and had one son, who gave him a grandson and granddaughter. Now at the age of 98 and a great-grandfather, he tells of his exploits at work and war.

Introduction

Hilton Kemp

Searchlight Operator on the Isle of Wight.
392 Searchlight Company.
Royal Engineers 48th Hampshire Territorials.

I first met Hilton 'online', some three years ago, while researching my book *'Culver Cliff and the Isle of Wight of War.'*

He kindly gave me many hours of his time to tell me the story of those hectic, desperate and dangerous times.

Recently, at 98 years of age, he asked if it would be possible to publish his complete memoirs. I was pleased to do it, at no cost, to thank him for his time, his infectious humour and his service.

I could write much more, But this is Hilton's story.

There was no ambiguity about the war.

The men and women who put their lives on the line were prepared to accept sacrifice. If necessary, the ultimate sacrifice, to protect their countries, their peoples, and their families, from a monstrous and evil tyranny.

We owe our peace and freedom today, to that readiness on their part. And for the sacrifice of so many. We salute them.

They changed our world, and they kept it safe.

Tim Wander, October 2019.

Contents

The Island

For anyone who is unacquainted with the Isle of Wight, here is a brief description of the locality where I originated.

The Garden Isle, as it is deservedly called, lies some 5 miles off of the southern central coast of England, opposite the busy ports of Southampton, and Portsmouth. The historic stretch of water called the Solent, divides it from the mainland.

There are always ships yachts and vessels of all descriptions plying to and fro. Almost diamond shaped, the Island is some 23 miles from east to west, and about 13 miles from north to south at its widest point, with a coastal area of 60 miles of sandy bays, intermingled with chalk and sand stone cliffs. In places these cliffs consist of multi- coloured sands, and the bones of dinosaurs are often found where the cliffs have fallen away, together with other fossils. The land area of 155 square miles, is of grassy Downs on which are rare wild orchids, wild flowers and butterflies, while migratory birds fly across from the continent and cattle and sheep graze peacefully, with the sparkling blue sea as a backwash to complete the picture.

Although the Island is mainly agricultural, there are 7 main towns, Newport the capital is centrally placed. There are several picturesque villages, many of the cottages with thatched roofs and even a thatched church. A fertile valley between the Downs is where acres of potatoes are grown, also tomatoes and flowers are especially cultivated in large green houses.

Boat building used to be the main industry, but now they make parts for helicopters and aircraft. The Hovercraft of course was invented here by Sir Christopher Cockerell in 1959, and a thriving industry resulted from it on the river Medina which flows through the town of Cowes so that there is East Cowes on one side and Cowes on the other, which boasts The Royal Yacht Squadron where Royalty arrive on the first week in August, known nationally as Cowes Week. Rich and famous personalities gather to participate in the yacht races and the general revelry that takes place during that week and quite a while afterwards. Osborne House at East Cowes was the home of Queen Victoria and Albert the Prince Consort. This imposing house and grounds is open to the fee paying public during the summer.

The Island was and still is a popular holiday resort, trains run from Waterloo station in London to Portsmouth, where the ferry runs across to Ryde, which has a very long pier because the tide recedes a long way out over the sands. There is a car ferry that sails across from Fishbourne to Portsmouth and a passenger ferry from Ryde pier, while the Hovercraft runs from Ryde esplanade terminus to Southsea. Likewise, ferries run across from Southampton to Cowes, the car ferry to East Cowes and the passenger ferry to Cowes. Then there is a car ferry from Yarmouth to Lymington which takes foot passengers as well. People seek to retire here, because of the clean healthy sea air, the slower pace of life, and the comparatively mild climate.

This then, I hope, sets the scene of my environment, to commence my narrative.

The Beginning

I was born on the 19th April 1921, in a small cottage in the seaside town of Ryde on the Isle of Wight. My earliest memories are of a happy household consisting of Mother, Father and my two sisters Elsie and Myra. Elsie was two years older than me and Myra was two years younger.

We had none of the 'mod-cons' that are taken for granted today, just basic necessities. The Island was a bit behind the times compared with the mainland, in fact the whole country was still in recession recovering from the first world war, employment was hard to find and wages were a mere pittance and most people were very poor, but proud and honest.

There was no Social Security, or National Health Service in those days, it was amazing how some people managed to survive on next to nothing. There were what we called odd characters about, trying to make a living as best they could, but there were no beggars and crime figures were low. An Italian organ grinder used to come round the streets and his barrow organ with a monkey on the top was pulled by a donkey, the monkey would turn somersaults for a penny.

The local fishermen used to hawk their catch around the streets on a barrow crying "Fresh herring oh! a penny each, 13 for a shilling!"
I should explain that there were 12 pennies to a shilling. The catch varied according to the season and often it was sprats or mackerel, whatever was

about at the time. They would be followed down the street by the local cats, as the fish was gutted and filleted as they went.

Those were the days of gas lamps, coal fires and chimney sweeps. There was also the Ash man, whose job it was to clear the ashes of the fire from the ash pit at the back of the house. Ours was a picturesque little Irish man who wore a green round hat, with a narrow brim and a clay pipe stuck in the hat band. His corduroy trousers were "yorked up" as we called it, with a strap below each knee. He used to come along at a leisurely pace with his horse and cart. I think that his name was Pat Mahoney.

Salty Sally was a little old lady who used to sell salt from door to door, she had the appearance of a witch, with only two teeth, one at the top and one at the bottom, the local wags used to declare that she couldn't eat pickled onions, because she couldn't catch them. My mother was horrified once to see her take a sweet from her mouth and offer it to my baby sister in her pram.

The Watercress man had a plaintive cry to advertise his wares which the kids would mimic as he wandered from town to town all over the island. Happy Harry was an ex public school type, who wore an open necked shirt summer and winter, he sported a beard and always had a buttonhole flower of some kind, he would bathe in the sea every day of the year, regardless of the weather. His hobby was attending auction sales, where he would out bid genuine dealers and buyers just for the hell of it, he had no interest in his purchases and after having them delivered and dumped in his back garden, would leave them to rot. When the pile was so big that it became a nuisance to the neighbours, he would have it removed to the dump.

There were hardly any motor cars or vans in those days and trades people used either a horse and cart a hand cart, or an errand boy's carrier bicycle to make their deliveries. Consequently, children could play their ball games etc.' safely in the street, sometimes having a skipping rope right across the street for all to join in.

Toys were very simple home made things. I remember having a little peddle car which was made for me by a next door neighbour, who was a mechanic, it was my pride and joy although it was very simply made. Clockwork toys mostly made in Germany needed no batteries of course. Another favourite toy was an iron hoop, used with the aid of an iron hook. I remember that mine broke once and Dad took me and the broken hoop along to the local blacksmith to have it repaired.

The Blacksmith played a big part in the community in those days and apart from shoeing horses, would undertake all sorts of jobs to do with metal work like repairing farm implements and making gates etc. I was fascinated to see him at work with the large bellows blowing the fire into white hot heat. I nosed around at the pieces of farm machinery and things that were scattered about the place.

On the wall at the back of the forge there was a dart board under which four old men sat playing cards. I suppose that the old chaps used the forge as a meeting place as it was always warm in there.

Speaking of warm places, just as there was a pub in almost every street, so there were many small bakeries, there was one in our street and we would listen to the crickets singing and chirping as we stood outside enjoying the aroma of fresh baked bread. The baker would deliver the bread from a brightly painted hand cart. People used to grow as many vegetables as they could and allotments were in great demand. We kids used to collect horse manure and leaves in the autumn in our hand carts which we would push down to the allotments glad to be doing our little bit to help. These hand carts consisted of a wooden box on a set of pram wheels, with a piece of batten nailed to each side for handles and they were quite sturdy.

We had what we called a trolley as well, which consisted of a wooden box nailed onto a long board with a pair of pram wheels at the front and back the front axle would be on a swivel to give movement for steerage with a piece of rope each end tied behind each wheel like reins to steer with, and our street being on a hill, we had lots of fun with that. We even had a brake on it, which was a piece of wood for a lever on the side of the box with a block on the bottom end to rub on the wheel when the lever was pulled. Pocket money didn't exist, it was a red letter day if we had a penny given to us, and if we wanted cash we had to earn it. Most people kept live stock in their back gardens, such as poultry, rabbits and pigeons, not as pets I hasten to add, but for the table. A chicken dinner was considered a luxury and a common meal was rabbit stew with dumplings that was before the awful myxomatosis disease that affected rabbits was heard of. We youngsters used to collect old bones from the chicken runs and together with jam jars, rabbit skins and rags, sell them to the rag and bone man for a few pennies. A penny was made up of four farthings so that we could buy four small items such as sherbet dabs, aniseed balls, tiger nuts and bulls eyes. We made our own amusements and in their seasons we played French cricket, conkers, marbles, top and whip, bows and arrows and catapults. On one great occasion I was presented with a real leather football that mother had obtained by saving Oxo coupons and suddenly I was a very popular chap, actually having a real football! One of my prize possessions before graduating to a second hand bike was a kiddy's scooter and I had lots of fun with that, as our street was on quite a steep hill. Air guns were popular and I eventually managed to save up enough to buy one. I became quite a good shot, this was advantageous, as our school master lived only four houses away from us and I was able to get my own back on him by shooting up his glass case, the sort that would cover a stuffed bird, which he foolishly kept on the roof of his shed.

We didn't get into any real mischief, although one episode lives in my memory. We used to play football in the street with old tennis balls, just a group of young lads having a kick about. As a rule, people were pretty tolerant if a ball went into their front gardens and would allow us to recover it without any fuss, but two old spinster sisters lived together in one house and their front garden like all the others was small with a low wall topped by iron railings, with an iron gate. They used to have a padlock and chain on the gate and would keep watch behind net curtains to see if our ball went into their garden, if it did, they would not return it, they would rush out to get it refusing to throw it back and scolding us for playing football in the street and saying that they were going to burn the ball. That ball was lost for good and unless another could be found that was the end of our game.

We agonized over this, wondering what could be done about it, until one day we came up with a brain wave. I obtained a shotgun cartridge from my uncle's farm and we removed the shot, the gunpowder charge was then put into an old split tennis ball and the split sealed up. We started playing and of course the ball was quite accidentally kicked over the railings into the old ladies' front garden. True to form one of them rushed out to retrieve it, by the way it was always the same sister than ran out no doubt aided and abetted by the other. They had a coal fire burning and the chimney was smoking nicely as we retreated further up the road to watch events, we didn't have long to wait, there was a muffled boom and a mushroom of smoke puffed out of the chimney, seconds later the sisters ran out calling for help, but there wasn't a child in sight. Shortly after this there was a policeman at our door enquiring about the incident, I remember my mother getting quite indignant with him at the thought of her son being involved in such a thing, naturally she was blissfully unaware of the part that I had played. I rather fancy that the padlock came off after that, but in truth I don't recall.

Living as we did by the seaside meant that during the summer months we could spend most of our time on the beach. Mother would provide us with a packet of sandwiches and a bottle of lemonade and we would happily spend the whole day there. Our first job on arrival would be to dig a large hole in the sand with seats cut into the sides, big enough for three or four children to use as their base, or house as we called it for the day, but we always filled it in on leaving for home, as the tide covered it and it would have been dangerous to paddling kiddies.

There were various buskers on the beach trying to earn a few coppers from the holiday makers, but we kids enjoyed the entertainment for nothing. Together with all the other locals we knew the patter of the traditional Punch and Judy show. There was a ventriloquist who had a man sized dummy called Laddie which wore a decent suit and bow tie and had jointed arms and legs enabling it to walk stiffly supported by "The Governor" as he was called. He could make the dummy cry spurting water from Laddie's eyes all over the audience. When we heard the cry "Here comes Laddie" we would follow him along the beach and settle down to hear his spiel although we knew it almost word perfect from constant repetition. There was also a trio with a banjo, violin and guitar they would play and sing on the beach and then go round with the hat. It was useless to feign sleep because the collector would wave his cap under your nose until you paid up. Once they had collected enough they would head for the nearest pub across the road, and spend the proceeds.

As well as the buskers there were various people selling things from trays around their necks along the esplanade, they were untroubled by traffic which only consisted of horse drawn landaus and an occasional motor omnibus or charabanc.

The sight of majestic liners passing by on their way into or out of Southampton docks was commonplace and hardly caused any comment, except perhaps to discuss which one it was, or what line she belonged to, we could tell by the ships lines or the number of her funnels what her name was, we knew them all at a glance. Alas they no longer exist since air travel has made them obsolete, except for the occasional cruise liner. Also of course, Portsmouth being a great naval base, warships of various types were seen passing to and fro, and the review of the fleet was a great occasion, being attended by the Royal Yacht and dressed over all with bunting.

The huge millionaire's yachts that sailed the Solent in those days were a splendid sight, but caused no envy, in our innocence they belonged to a world of opulence beyond our comprehension. We knew nothing of drugs, violence and crime and sex was a mystery unknown to us and never mentioned in the presence of children. Therefore, we were not afraid to talk to strangers and never felt the need to lock our doors at night, or chain up a bicycle, also babies could be safely left outside the house or shop in their prams.

There was no colour prejudice simply because there were no coloured people, at least not in our area. When at last I graduated to owning a second hand bike, my world expanded and I discovered places hitherto beyond my reach, in consequence relatives who until now had been secluded, found that they were invaded by my pals and I, breaking new ground.

Uncle Ern's Farm

Mothers brother, Uncle Ern., had a dairy farm just a few miles out of the town. He had a son named Arthur, who was about my age and four daughters. Arthur and I spent most of our spare time together doing all the things that boys do in the country. We climbed every tree and rigged swings from their branches. We endeavoured to help with the work about the farm, but often got into more trouble than our help was worth. Cowboy films were all the rage at the cinema and we used to go to the Saturday afternoon matinees, for a few pence, then we would try to re-enact the scenes back at the farm. We would play Cowboys and Indians with our cap guns, bows and arrows and stock whips, we would even lasso the heifers if we could. Peggy the work horse was our cow pony and not having any riding tack we simply put on the bridle and rode her bare back. They also had a Billy goat which we would hitch up to our hand cart and use it as a chariot.
Arthur was very knowledgeable about birds and their habits and we studied them, getting to recognize their individual songs and calls. A popular sport was rabbiting because they represented food and pocket money, with snares and ferrets. We also set mole traps as moleskins could be sold for sixpence each and that was good money! I remember when Woolworth Stores first opened in our town selling nothing over sixpence, showing the

value of moleskins, which we used to nail to the stable door to cure them. Mushrooms too could be sold to the shopkeepers for pocket money, as I said, if you wanted pocket money, you had to earn it. This was no bad thing as it taught us the value of money and that it doesn't grow on trees.

Arthur and I used to go for long cycle rides on our "bone shakers" as we used to call them, as some of the gravel roads were very rough and bumpy and we would attempt to go all around the island in one day, the terrain was very hilly and we didn't have the low gears used today. We often came a "cropper," usually ending up with grazed knees since all school boys wore short trousers then. One day we were riding quite fast down a steep country lane, I was in front and rounding a bend my front wheel hit a rock lying in the road. I shot over the handlebars and Art who was unable to avoid me, crashed into me and knocked himself unconscious. We were miles from anywhere, so I dragged him to the grass verge and tried to revive him while wondering what to do next, when I was relieved to see a car coming up the hill towards us. The kindly driver took him to hospital, while I pushed the bikes back home and had to explain everything to our worried parents. We didn't have telephones so I had to go over to the farm and inform them. He was unconscious for seven long anxious days, but fortunately suffered no permanent damage.

As boys of course we were fascinated by water, not the washing kind I might add! We spent many happy hours on the banks of streams and ponds with homemade nets and jam jars studying the pond life. We tried our hand at fishing both fresh water and salt, we made our own tackle and got by with hand lines, we couldn't afford sophisticated rods and reels. How lucky we were to be able to enjoy both the seaside and the country, we learnt a lot about nature by just playing and observing our surroundings, or keeping quite quiet and still to observe the more timid creatures.

The kites that we made were simple affairs using whatever materials came to hand, like split cane, brown paper and string. While flying them I recall that on windy days during the summer, for instance in the August holidays, being fascinated by the ever changing shapes of the huge white cumulus clouds, against the blue background of the sky, or the different types of cloud formations those known as Mares tails denoting a high wind, or Herringbone pattern a gentle breeze etc.. There were no overhead wires to worry about, but we often got tangled up in the trees and had to climb up to free them. This was all part of the fun, for we were as agile as monkeys and very proficient at tree climbing.

Life was not all fun and games as we did what we could to help about the farm, like the never ending mucking out, haymaking and a whole host of other chores. Art used to complain that his father only had one hand, as the other one was always holding his pipe!

Aunty Emma, his mother was small and petite, but worked as hard as any man, while caring for the house and bringing up the children, she also looked after the poultry and ran the dairy which involved running the milk through the cooler and separator to extract the cream for making butter the old fashion way, cranking the butter churn by hand. This was like a tub long ways on a stand with paddles inside it and a trap door opening and a cranking handle at the back, to revolve the churn until the butter is made. It is then taken out and patted into half pound or 250 gram blocks with wooden pats which looked like little cricket bats. Uncle Ern sold his milk round the houses, at first from a horse and trap and then from a motorbike and sidecar, He would dip up the milk from the churn with a metal measure and pour it into the customer's jug, that was how it was done before milk bottles came into use.

Once when passing an old hollow oak tree, Art dared me to climb up it, he knew that there was a barn owls nest in the top in a hollow, but I didn't, eventually I came face to face with a very angry owl that hissed at me and flew off with a great fluttering of wings. It frightened the life out of me and Art of course was doubled up with mirth at the fact that I had been caught out. Speaking of trees, I should mention that in our youth there were great majestic Elm trees which grew very tall, with wide spreading branches, giving shade for the cattle and favourite nesting places for rookeries, alas they are all gone now, killed off by the "Dutch Elm" disease as it was called, completely altering the appearance of the landscape in most places. We sadly miss their beauty and hope that they will be restored in years to come.

On rainy days we would play in the great barn with our marbles and cigarette cards, all the lads collected them and we would swap with each other to make them up into sets of all kinds, like pictures of birds, butterflies, film stars, cricketers, footballers, ships, cars, wild flowers and many more. We could buy five cigarettes for tuppence (=two pence) and had our first crafty puffs. We didn't like it, but got a kick out of it just because it was forbidden.

Harvest time was always a very busy time for everyone and although it was hard work we had a lot of fun trying to help. The threshing machine was driven by a steam engine with a tall chimney stack and a big flywheel and we were warned to keep well clear of the long driving belt. Our job was a simple one standing the bundles of corn up in bundles known as stooks, five bundles per stook if I remember correctly. As the cutter and binder went round in ever decreasing circles getting closer to the centre of the field, the rabbits that were in that patch of corn got ready to bolt as it got smaller and smaller, then we would gather round with sticks or "knobby joes" as we called them in the hope of hitting one as they bolted.

Every time that a rabbit rushed out of the corn, a wild cheer would go up to spur it on its way. Some rabbits were caught this way, but most escaped, having caused us much amusement and laughter at all the banter and excitement that went on. Those that were killed were laid out in a line and divided among the workers, who were pleased to receive them, for they made a good dinner for the family.

The Old Water Mill

My favourite season of the year is spring time, after enduring the dreary winter, it is so delightful to notice the days getting longer, the sun getting warmer and most of all to hear the birds singing their dawn chorus.

I was fortunate in having an Uncle who was the Miller at an old water mill; this mill is so old that it was mentioned in the Doomsday book of 1086. It was situated deep in the country, in a picturesque setting and we children would sometimes stay there during the summer holidays. They had four children of their own, so that we were able to play together. When we visited there, we were entering another era so to speak. They were almost completely self-sufficient regarding food. Uncle Alf kept pigs, poultry and bees and had a large garden with two brooks running through it, where we fished for sticklebacks. The beehives were under the apple trees and uncle grew prize vegetables and flowers which he used to show. In fact, he was such an expert that he was a judge at the village shows and of course we used to go too. He was also a keen sportsman playing cricket for the local team. At the side of the mill there were stables, where the landlord kept his fine hunter horses.

On Sundays we would all go off to Sunday school, walking to the village about two miles away, although to us it seemed much further, the little ones being urged on by the older children fearful of being late. We wore cheap black canvas sand shoes with no socks so that we often had painful blisters on our heels through hurrying along, but that didn't merit any sympathy. I remember the song of the Yellow hammers in the hedges all along the lanes. (A little bit of bread and no cheese) was our interpretation of their song, you may have heard the jingle. Chicken and ducks had to be penned up every evening safe from the foxes and let out again first thing in the morning, to forget to do that could be catastrophic.

When you entered the mill through a heavy oak plank door, with a big iron old fashioned lock and a large wooden latch in the shape of an arm that dropped into a groove, with a cord going through a hole above to the other side with a toggle on the end, which was pulled to lift the latch from that side, you are stepping back in time, to old oak beams and wooden machinery. The old mill used to rumble and shake as the huge wooden waterwheel slowly turned; driving the large wooden cogwheels geared up to the grind stone and a film of white flour dust covered everything.

There was a chain that came right down through the three floors through hinged trap doors which were in two halves with a hole in the middle for the chain to pass through, this was to haul sacks of grain up to the other floors, as the sack came up to the trap doors they would open upwards as it passed through and then drop down into position again. Although we were warned to keep away from the machinery, we couldn't resist setting this in motion when there was no one about, grabbing the chain and being hauled up to the top floor! The farmers would bring the grain in their carts and it was fascinating for us "Townies" to listen to their talk, for they had a strong brogue which sadly is fast disappearing. The ground corn and crushed maze was delivered to the farms by lorry and we would pester the driver to let us ride in the back through the winding country lanes. This was a special treat to us as there were not many motor vehicles about at that time. In fact, to get from our house to the mill a distance of about 15 miles, mother used to arrange for us to be picked up by carrier's van.

The Carrier was a man who earned his living by carrying and fetching goods from place to place for people in his little van. So with us cramped in the back, he would meander about the countryside, dropping off and picking up his deliveries. He was also a source of information passing on the latest scandal and snippets of gossip as he went on his way in a leisurely fashion. Our journey would take the best part of all day, but to us cramped as we were it was all part of the adventure. If someone wanted the carrier to call, they simply stuck a flag in the shape of a piece of rag tied to a stick in the hedge in full view. I am glad to say that the old mill is still standing to this day, though it no longer rumbles and shakes, but stands still and silent. Long may it remain as a reminder of slower more peaceful days, but work was harder and more manual than it is today.

When I last visited there, I looked at that chain, and imagined that I was a mischievous "nipper" as we were called, being hauled up through those trap doors to the top floor strictly against orders.

Uncle had some breeding sows and we used to delight in watching them being fed and admiring the baby piglets. It was interesting too to watch him extracting the honey from the hives he used a smoke puffer a simple devise like a small bellows with a burner under it producing smoke which he would puff at the bees to make them docile while he extracted the honeycomb made on to a frame and he had a simple machine called a "Separator", the frames of honeycombs were slotted inside and the handle was turned as fast as possible so that the honey was thrown out by centrifugal force and collected in a container at the bottom. At one time they used to kill a pig and salt it down, there were large metal hooks fastened to the kitchen beams to hang up the hams for smoking.

The toilet came as a shock to the uninitiated, as it was simply a bucket under a wooden seat in a little lavatory at the back of the house. You had to go up a slope and round the corner, so it was referred to by the delicate phrase of "Up round".

I have very fond memories of, the jolly miller, playing French cricket and football with us, whenever he got the chance. He possessed many skills which were essential in his day, but are now obsolete and have faded out of use.

School

The school that I attended was the local church school, it was a two story stone built place with four classrooms, there were two entrances one for boys and one for girls, the sexes were also segregated by a high stone wall between the playgrounds.

There were none of the modern appliances that are taken for granted today, a coal fire was the only heating in each room and of course in cold weather this was monopolized by the teacher.

We sat at two seater desks facing the front, using steel nibbed pens dipped into the inkwells that were sunk into the desks. The main lessons were the "three Rs" as they were known, consisting of reading, writing and arithmetic with several other subjects such as history geography, art, science, singing, woodwork for the boys and cooking for the girls and PT which stood for physical training. Discipline was strict; the cane was very much in evidence and accepted by us as a matter of course. The teachers on reflection were quite decent types, considering what they had to put up with, but they were never very tolerant and I cannot recall any amusing incidents that occurred, although there must have been some. There was one instance I recall when an irate mother having an argument with the teacher declared that she would sue him for "definition" of character. Conditions were very basic, for instance, having no gymnasium, our PT consisted of physical jerks outside and running round the playground. In the absence of any public swimming pool, we had to learn to swim in the sea.

We had singing lessons sometimes, but there was no piano, so we had to make do with a tuning fork. For woodwork and cookery lessons we had to go to another premises known as the School of Art. I always looked forward to woodwork as it was a change from the normal, as was Art, we would take objects like wild flowers and autumn leaves, or berries to school and try to copy them using watercolours.

School dinners hadn't come into being and there were no school buses, everyone walked or cycled to school in all weathers, some had long distances to travel but parents didn't consider it necessary to escort them, there were no perverts preying on children then and not much fear of being run over. The boys were mostly rough types whose normal entertainment was fighting, wrestling and ball games, one had to be tough to be one of the gang. One of our greatest fears was the school dentist, who had to be seen to be believed, the poor chap had been wounded in the First World War, causing him to drag his leg behind him in to us a most frightening manner, he was also very short of patience and tact. The dentist drill was worked by a foot pedal which made it slow and painful and the anaesthetics didn't seem to be strong enough, compared with how they are today. For complicated extractions we had to go to the hospital where we were given gas. Some of the kids were so scared by this chap, that it put them off dentists for life!

Starting Work

Like most boys at that time who were around the age of about 13 years, I got a job as an errand boy for the local butcher on Saturdays for a small wage, plus usually a pound of sausages as well, to help out with the family income. The carrier bike had a small wheel in the front and a large carrier to hold a big basket, which when loaded up would tip the bike up unless you leaned on the saddle to hold it down. There were times when this happened of course and then some customers got the wrong orders, because the labels got mixed up and it was difficult for a boy to sort out one from the other, but we got by somehow.

There was one house I remember, where we were requested to always leave the meat in the outside toilet, on the lavatory seat! But often when people were out at work, or not at home, they would expect us to walk in and leave the meat on the kitchen table, so trusting were they in those days. I learned how to bone and prepare the meat and make sausages. They had their own farm where they fattened cattle and did their own slaughtering, which is against the law now and I used to avoid going there unless I had to, not wishing to get involved in those activities. The butcher was a cheerful sort of chap, who would pass uncomplimentary comments about the customers behind their backs, only in fun of course, to cause a chuckle.

Our local grocer also gave me a job as errand boy in the evenings, especially during the Christmas period. On approaching the school leaving age of 14, my father and I had the anxious task of finding me full time employment which at that time was by no means easy. However, I eventually had interviews for two jobs and was accepted for both. One was for 5 years' apprenticeship as a gas fitter at the local gas company and the other as a shop assistant in a wine shop run by the brewery.

The gas company seemed the best option, knowing that if one was satisfactory, there was a job for life, so I was to be taken on for a month's trial, on 1-8-1935 I never did learn if I was satisfactory, even after 48 years' service. As I was 14 on the 19th April 1935, I duly left school at the start of the school holidays on the 1st of August in that year, and started work that day. I well remember turning up on my bike in time for when the hooter went at 7.30 am, for if you arrived late, they docked half an hour from your meagre wages. So there I was in my new bib and brace overalls, feeling shy and lost and not knowing what was expected of me and there was no reception committee, in fact no one seemed to bother. I was eventually put in the stores to learn the names of the fittings, appliances, parts and components, under the store-man a kindly old pipe smoking ex-naval man, who used to encourage me to "loose myself" as he put it when times were slack. Our hours were from 7.30 am until 12 noon and 1 pm until 5 pm with half a day off on Saturdays. We had one week's annual holiday. After a few weeks in the stores I was sent out with a fitter to learn the trade. Some were harder taskmasters than others, but the "nipper" always got the dirty jobs, but as a rule they were not a bad bunch.

There was a gang of labourers for digging holes in the road with picks and shovels, to deal with leaks or run mains and services. In an emergency we would be called on to help out, this could be at night in all weathers and conditions. This situation did not occur very often fortunately, but we were paid overtime when it did. I wonder what those chaps would think if they could see all the technology used to do the job today. There was an office at the end of the stores, where the fitters wrote out their time sheets and received their orders for the day; also any parts needed from the stores were drawn across a counter at the end of the office. While this was going on, the boys were kept busy cleaning and sharpening tools and cutting threads on pipes, we were never allowed to be idol; if there was nothing to do we had to sweep the floor, or pretend to be busy, even if we weren't.

These were the days of coal gas and there was not much electric lighting, the streets were lit by gas and in our small town there were four lamplighters who each had their own section of the town to attend to. They would clean and adjust the street lamps during the day, then in the evening they went round with a long pole with a flame on the end fed by carbide gas, which they used to turn on and light the lamps and then in the morning they had to put them out again. Eventually the lamps had clocks and pilot lights fitted so that they would come on and off automatically, but they still had to be checked up on to make sure that they were all alight. New houses being built, were fitted up with iron pipes from the meter, with points to the cooker, fire, water heater, etc..

We boys had the arduous task of cutting the channels in the brickwork, or chasing as it was called, so that the pipes could be hidden behind the plaster. We didn't wear gloves or goggles, as protective clothing was unheard of and often the hammer would slip and strike your hand. It is a fact that in my time, two chaps each lost an eye through a chip flying off of the end of the chisel. The boys also had the job of measuring up, cutting the pipes to length and screwing a thread on each end, with a tool called stocks and dies, this was hard work and needed muscle power. Geysers were fitted using lead pipes and we wiped the joints using a paraffin plumber's blowlamp. A gas fitters blow lamp is different, it is simply a piece of brass tube about one inch in diameter and about six inches long, blanked off at the base and a wick made of rag at the top. It is filled with methylated spirit and the flame is regulated by a thin tube clipped to the side of the large tube, with a length of rubber tube held in the mouth to blow the flame forward, we used to make our own. It is tricky to use under the floor boards, as the spirit is apt to leak. The pipes that we used for gas work were made of a combination of lead and zinc known as Compo, and we had to carry it in rolls on the handle bars of our bikes, together with heavy tool bags. It was known for the front forks to break under the strain, but the bike was our property, and we couldn't claim any damages. Lead piping is now banned of course and substituted by copper. We had to supply our own tools, and they could be costly, some were handmade and some were bought second hand, steel chisels were made from old files and tempered by the blacksmith. There were none of the power tools that are taken for granted today, it was all muscle power, and holes were drilled by brace and bit and punched through walls with steel chisels. Often they were stone walls and very thick. By the way our tool bags were often made from an old carpet sewn to shape, with rope handles.

I got friendly with the blacksmith at our works, he was a Devonshire ex-cavalry farrier, and very clever with metal work of all sorts. One day I walked into the forge and seeing a shaped piece of metal on the floor, I picked it up but I jolly soon dropped it again, he had just thrown it down after working it from red hot. My hand was badly burned, and I yelled, he immediately grabbed my wrist in a vice like grip, and trying to reassure me blew up his fire holding my hand over the heat. I kicked and struggled and protested in vain. He held me there saying it's alright son, the fire will thaw out the burn, this didn't make any sense to me, but he knew what he was about and sure enough it worked. My hand was cured and I suffered no ill effects.

The old fashioned gas fires used to be fitted in front of a thick asbestos surround which we had to saw to shape, breathing in the dust, we also used to lag hot water pipes with it, we hadn't heard of asbestosis then, but we weren't affected by it. When fitting gas fires in old stately homes, we often had to clear out the sticks and rubbish deposited in the chimneys by rooks and jackdaws. Almost everyone smoked in those days, it was the accepted thing to do, some took snuff, and some chewed tobacco and some even did all three of those things.

A wizened little cockney fitter that I worked with used to chew "baccy", and after wiping a lead joint he would spit a stream of baccy juice on it to cool it down and the smell was very unpleasant! Some were chain smokers and one chap who always seemed to have a dewdrop on the end of his nose, would smoke the "fag" right down until the dewdrop dripped on it and sizzled! One old chain smoking clerk used to let the fag ash fall on his ledger and write on through it as though it wasn't there.

We used to have to work in all sorts of places, ordinary houses, hotels and cafes, flats and doss houses; we certainly saw some odd places. There was an Abbey near Ryde, and also a Nunnery, and when working in there, we were able to enter a room, but if we closed the door behind us weren't able to come out again, it locked automatically, and we had to ring a bell, and wait to be let out. Once as a young boy, our job was down in the dimly lit crypt which consisted of a series of archways and pillars. I was up a ladder working and I happened to look down and saw a monk in a white habit with his cowl pulled up slowly walking out from behind an alcove with his hands together in the praying position I was so startled that I nearly fell off of the ladder!

Joining the Territorial Army

I was friendly with a lad, named Ernest, who was in the Salvation Army and played the euphonium, his brother played the cornet, and his father who was the band master also played the cornet and I used to go to some of their meetings, but I wouldn't join, however we were good friends. His father was also in the Territorial Army and used to tell us about the good times that he had at the annual camp and kidded us about joining up, but we were too young at that time to do so.
We used to listen to the big brass bands on the wireless and I had a chance to learn music, but alas wasn't interested enough to do so. Even so it made me aware of the pleasure one gets from listening to music and I sometimes would listen to the band playing on the esplanade in the band stand, those were pleasant peaceful days and we hadn't a care in the world. As time passed there was much unrest in Germany. The National Socialist Party

had come to power, led by a megalomaniac named Adolf Hitler, an ugly little man with a Charley Chaplin moustache but there was nothing funny about him. He recruited, gangs of vicious thugs called Blackshirts or Nazis who terrorized the population into submission to do his will and no one dare resist or speak out against him on pain of imprisonment or even death in a concentration camp. He built up the armed forces thus creating employment and improving living standards, so that he was well thought of by the German people at the time, but he had an ulterior motive, his aim was to gain territory and he began taking over neighbouring countries. In order to finance these things, he terrorized the Jews, humiliating them at first then evicting them from their homes, robbing them of their possessions putting them into concentration camps and finally murdering them.

He coveted Poland and our Prime Minister Neville Chamberlain a quiet level headed man tried to reason with him to no avail and it looked as though war was imminent, but to us such a thing was unthinkable, we the British were totally unprepared, having totally demobilized since the last Great War. Of course Hitler knew that and he was out to avenge us for Germany's defeat in that war.

We lads being at a carefree age didn't bother ourselves much about politics and used to laugh it off saying "Cheer up it may never happen" and in fact never dreamed that it would happen in our lifetime, but never the less we couldn't entirely ignore what was so obvious, every news reel at the cinema, showed Hitler ranting and raving at mass military rallies and every news program on the wireless gave out the same sort of thing. Ern's father old Reg still kept chatting us up about joining the Territorials and so we decided to do so and duly turned up for our medicals. Ern didn't pass but I did, so he was out, and I was in. So I joined the 48th Anti-Aircraft Battalion, Royal Engineers 392 Searchlight Company on the 26-1-1939. Our uniforms and equipment was very much of the 1914 to 1918 type, except for the knee length puttees. My comrades were a mixture of tradesmen, some were old soldiers, veterans of the last war and knew what it was all about, but the majority were youngsters like myself, who thought that they knew it all, but were as green as grass and cocky with it. Of course we didn't worry about the future and hadn't an inkling of what lay ahead.

When an Officer asked"What is that man's name?" Indicating me I was quite thrilled, because one was not considered to be a man until the age of 21 in those days in civvy street, but you were in the army, from the age of 18 and I was three months short of 18.

I can never forget our first rifle drill with fixed bayonets for the new recruits, fortunately we were in open order, there was a very short chap in the front row and on the command slope arms, he threw the rifle up his right side and across to his left shoulder with such vigour that it shot over his shoulder and the bayonet stuck in the floor with the butt swaying to and fro only inches in front of the nose of the chap behind him. While we all struggled to keep straight faces the drill sergeant "tore him off a strip"!

Months passed and the sabre rattling in Germany got worse. Every time the wireless was switched on there was this "Windbag" Hitler screaming his head off! We realized that he was not kidding and that war was a real possibility.

War is Declared

On the 8th August 1939, an officer called at my home asking for me, my mother took a dim view of this turn of events and rudely told him that if he wanted me he would have to go and look for me. I was at work and when I arrived back at the works preparatory to knocking off, a clerk called through the office window "Hey the king wants you, you're called up!"

I went home to change into uniform and reported to the drill hall with all my kit. To use the official phraseology, our call up was for a month's embodiment. Little did we know it but that month turned into six and a half years of war service. I was demobilized on the 21st March 1946. It didn't end there, because I was called up again on the 27th April 1952 on what was called Z Reserve owing to the Suez Canal crisis, but it only lasted for two weeks until the 11th May. I enjoyed that little break up at Stiffkey in Norfolk and this time I was the old soldier but that is another story.

Those war years were a great adventure, I travelled far and wide taking the rough with the smooth and thank God that I lived to tell the tale, there were many times when I thought that I wouldn't survive but I was one of the lucky ones. I have often reminded myself of that fact when times have been hard and I think of my comrades who were not so lucky.

Our searchlight company was stationed on the Island at first which was fortunate for us when it came to going on leave and friends used to say "Hello! On leave again then, when are you going back?" What they meant was "How long have you got?" But it sounded as though they wanted to get rid of us, this was a standing joke and we used to laugh about it. Things were much more complicated as regards getting home to the Island on leave once I was posted to the mainland; meanwhile we continually trained hard at our prospective jobs, although first off we were very short of arms and equipment of all sorts. Our army the British Expeditionary Force, or B.E.F. as it was called, was fighting in France, and of course took priority on stores, so that at first we used to go on guard, armed with only a pickaxe handle and five rounds of ammunition! We used to say "What are we supposed to do with the five rounds? Throw it at them?" Gradually things improved, and we began to receive our arms. Searchlights were apt to be sighted on high ground, giving a clear field of vision and often overlooking the sea as well, so that they could be used for coastal defence, as well as anti-aircraft, so that they were draughty places catching the wind.

First off we slept in bell tents on the ground, about 10 men or more to a tent, together with all our equipment. We were issued with bedding boards and a palisade. The bedding boards consisted of 2 cross pieces of wood about 4 inches wide and 2 feet six inches long. These went at the head and foot and on them was laid three boards side by side, with the paillasse, stuffed with straw laid on them for a mattress, this was our bed and it raised us about five or six inches off of the ground. We had a ground sheet which could be converted into a cape and 2 or 3 blankets, plus of course our great coats on top in the winter.

We mounted a guard or air sentry as he was called, constantly all round the clock, which usually meant 2 hours on and four off for those on guard duty, our slang word for this duty was going Stag of course this went on in all weathers day and night. We used to go in batches to headquarters or HQ, by lorry for lectures, square bashing or to go sick and we always sang our heads off going along. The popular songs at the time were Red sails in the sunset, "South of the Border" and "Deep Purple to name but a few. Being young we were carefree and light-hearted and laughed a lot, we thought that we were invulnerable if we thought about our fate at all. The same old jokes still caused a chuckle, like "Halt who goes there?" "Army Chaplain!" "Advance Charlie Chaplin and be recognized!" Or the verbal message passed down the line, "Hard pressed on the left send up reinforcements, "which ended up as "Hard up on the left send up three and four pence!" = three shillings and four pence in old money.

When the searchlight was on at night they used to chaff each other about climbing up the beam saying no fear, knowing you lot you would wait until I was half way up, and then switch it off. We didn't see much action at first, just an occasional enemy spotter plane, meanwhile the powers that be, decided that as searchlights were anti-aircraft, we must change over from Royal Engineers to Royal Artillery. Light Anti-Aircraft or Ack-Ack for short. This caused a big protest but to no avail. So having once been Sappers we were now Gunners, so our brass badges, buttons and collar dogs had to be changed and shortly after that we were issued with battle dress.

From the outset a strict blackout was enforced, anyone showing the smallest glimmer of light, was immediately told about it and persistent offenders were fined. Even so people could still walk the streets in perfect safety with no fear of being molested, as mugging simply was not done, in fact no such word existed. Our training was very extensive, now that we were artillery we had to learn Bofors gun drills, this was difficult as we had no gun, so we had to use our imagination and make a mock up Bofors gun, we had to use two forms placed across each other forming a cross, the traverse and elevation operators termed numbers 1 and 2, would sit at each end of the transverse form, while the firing and loading number 3 stood in the centre. Our (Gun) was now manned, now there were pretend ammunition numbers 4, and 5 bringing up the shells and setting the fuses.

This was all serious stuff, now the numbers 1 and 2 would have to sit up very alert turning their imaginary handles, sighting on to the target and reporting "On target" and on the command Fire, the number 3 would go through the motions of stamping his foot on the firing pedal, at the same time feeding clips of shells into the breech hopper and numbers 4 and 5 brought up the imaginary ammunition. We used to chuckle about this play acting, although it had to be taken seriously at the time, and as it turned out wasn't so stupid as it seemed, being not so different from the real thing as we discovered when at last we had the actual gun. We also had to learn infantry tactics, like hand to hand bayonet fighting, skirmishing and patrolling.

Funny things used to occur during these exercises. On one occasion our officer Captain Dell nicknamed "Dinky" announced that he intended to go to the top of a hill, a mile or so away and we had to stalk and capture him having taken him by surprise. Our approach was to be invisible to him. This was taking place on the Island and he wasn't an Island man, but our sergeant patrol leader was, as well as being an old soldier and crafty with it. He happened to know the farmer whose land the hill was on and he asked the dispatch rider to nip over to the farmer, mention the sergeant's name, tell him what was happening and ask him if he could distract the officer's attention at 12 noon. Off went the dispatch rider on his motorbike, before Dinky had left in the staff car. We had to travel on foot which would give Dinky plenty of time to get there. We knew that the ration lorry was due soon so we waited for it and piled in under the canvas cover the sergeant asked the driver to drop us off by a roundabout route to near our destination, stopping in a wood to get off unseen. We were then able to kill time while the sergeant reconnoitred. At about the appointed time we skirmished through the gorse bushes and sure enough there was Dinky surrounded by several farm labourers laughing chatting and smoking, they (happened) to be going rabbiting and stopped for a chat keeping him in conversation while we crept up on him and took him by surprise. He marvelled at our approach and said what a jolly good show! Not a sign of recognition passed between the men and their mate the sergeant so well did they play their part, but they must have been bursting with laughter at the officer's expense.

This is the kind of thing that kept us chuckling and I can equate with the TV program "Dads Army." Once we were on an exercise that involved the Home Guard, they supposedly were the enemy wearing soft hats while we wore steel helmets, so anyone wearing soft hats was the enemy. I was guarding a cross road when along came a military policeman or red cap, so called because they always wore a red cap. So I challenged him and he protested that he had nothing to do with the exercise, but I wouldn't let him go saying that any mug could walk about in a red cap and I marched him into the guard room and into a cell until the exercise was over he was furious but I didn't care, chuffed that I had got one over on him while obeying orders.

We had been told that the rattle normally used as a gas alarm, for the purpose of this exercise, represented a machine gun, but apparently the "enemy" hadn't been told because when we opened up with our rattle machine gun they all donned their gas masks fearing a gas attack and when we informed them that they were dead, they protested that they hadn't been told that the gas rattle was supposed to be a machine gun and therefore as far as they were concerned they were not dead. Corporal Jones would have said "Don't Panic"! This sort of thing caused many a laugh at the stupidity of it all, but it was meant to be so very serious, as our lives depended on intensive training and being able to act instinctively, without having to think twice about it!

Indirectly and quite by accident, I had a personal insight into the type of Nazi atrocities that we had been reading about in the papers. I had a boil in my armpit which wasn't responding to treatment and had to go to a military hospital for treatment which involved having it lanced. The young man in the next bed to me answered with a strong guttural accent when I greeted him and I thought surely not, he can't be a German, but on asking him where he came from, he replied "I am a German and I am ashamed of it! "Obviously the next question was "What are you doing here then?" His English was so bad that it was difficult to understand him, but he explained that he had escaped from a concentration camp and was a convalescent. Making the most of my opportunity, I said surely a lot of the stuff that we read in the papers about Nazi brutality must be propaganda to put our backs up against them. Very emphatically he said" Oh no! You believe and multiply ten times and you will still not understand!" Then he showed me the marks of whip lashes on his back. He said "A friend who escaped with me will be visiting me soon, you will notice that he has his hands in his pockets, there is a reason for this, he will not want to do so, but I will ask him to show you his hands." Later on his friend came and sure enough he had his hands in his trouser pockets they were chatting away in German and then I noticed that his visitor appeared to be protesting about something, but he came to me and took his hands out of his pockets to show me his thumbs, which were cut through to the bone, he had been hung up with his hands behind his back with piano wire tied round his thumbs. I had read that this one of their favourite party tricks, but never dreamed that I would see the evidence with my own eyes. I would have liked to have heard their story but it was early days and they were in a highly emotional state, so it was kindest to leave well alone and dwell on other things.

Apparently there was a pioneer corps for foreign nationals that they could join if they wished. I hope that their story had a happy ending, I had to go to hospital on very few occasions, but it seems that whenever I did, I met some interesting characters. The enemy was advancing through Holland and Belgium into France, the roads were choked with refugees, who were being bombed by Stuka dive bombers causing havoc and preventing free movement of our troops. France capitulated and our army had to retreat to Dunkirk for evacuation, this was an epic achievement and a story in its own right. The Germans swarmed into France, which meant that they were just across the channel and an invasion of our shores was likely to be attempted, so our orders were to carry our rifles and 50 rounds of ammunition with us at all times even on leave, in case of enemy parachutists dropping in uninvited.

Now the air raids started in earnest and we were very much in action both night and day. Swarms of enemy bombers and fighters flew right across the Island to bomb Portsmouth and Southampton. There were barrage balloons like miniature airships made of fabric and filled with gas floating above the cities in the hope of preventing the planes from flying too low, or that they might collide with the cables, these were easily shot down by the fighters at times. Our fighters engaged the enemy and "Dog fights" as they were called ensued, it was a thrilling sight to watch them twisting and turning, leaving vapour trails in the sky during daylight hours, but at night we were very much in action, often all night without a break and then when at last we stood down dog tire it wasn't unusual to be told "You're on Stag!".

As history shows the gallant R.A.F, gradually won the Battle of Briton as it was called, and that put paid to Hitler's plans for invasion. Bombing of major cities continued especially at night, so we were constantly on the alert and in a state of readiness, we didn't fully undress when we went to bed, being ready to "take post" and rush into action at a moment's notice.

In my first car with sister, Myra.

With my Father, Mother and sisters at 78 Arthur Street, Ryde (Pre-war)

Freddie Golding and I, on leave in Calcutta (1943)

Cousin Arthur and I, with dogs at Burnt House Lane, Newport.

Royal Engineers (1940)

Calcutta (1943)

3.7" Anti-Aircraft Guns

Searchlight Projector Lens being adjusted.

Ryde Seafront Ralph Plummer on the left and me on the right, can't remember the others name.

1953 Suez Crisis Recall

Two mainland lads messing around at Chillerton Camp.

Moving the searchlight

Leaving the Island

One day I was called to HQ, and told that I was to be sent on a Gun Fitters course. Some "Smart Alec" in the records office had seen apprentice gas fitter on my records and the fitter bit was enough for him, the fact that my type of training as a pipe fitter wasn't what was required, didn't register with the pen pushers who try to organize these things. What was needed was Bench Fitters, an entirely different skill to my training, so that I was at a disadvantage from the start. I had to report to a training camp in Spennymore in County Durham of all places. This was going to be quite an adventure, as I had only left the unit once before, to attend a wireless operators course on the Isle of Ely in Buckinghamshire.

The trains at that time were always packed with troops and other service personal, there were few civilians, the seats were always full and people were standing in the corridors, or sitting on their kit bags in any odd space. There were posters everywhere saying "Is your journey really necessary?" "Careless talk costs lives," "Be like Dad keep Mum!" "Walls Have ears" and so on. As so often happened, I palled up with a chap who was going on the same course as me at the same place. We had to change trains at Darlington and while waiting for our connection went into the buffet for a cup of tea, I should mention that I hadn't met any "Geordies" up until then and didn't understand their brogue, so when the young lady serving us said "Hello lad what fettle?" I was completely flummoxed and said "He did." "He did what?" said she "Ordered the teas", said I. "No, that's not what I meant" she replied. I said "I'm sorry but I'm an ignorant southerner and don't understand." "Well how are you?" she said," alright thank you, but what did you mean?" "That is what I meant!" She yelled, a bit rattled by now.

I would like to say that I found the "Geordies" were the most hospitable and friendly people that I ever came across in the whole of my travels. There were many instances of kindness to service personal, for instance if you got on a bus, they wouldn't take your fare, you just sat there offering the money and the conductress would pass you by as though she hadn't seen you, I found this a bit embarrassing, but got used to it.

The first part of the course was bench fitting which was very interesting and lasted about a month and ended with an examination which I passed and became an artificer or tradesman and was issued with a brass hammer and tongs to be worn on the left arm. We then had a free day off and while standing about on the street corner passing the time away, a smart young lady came over to me and said in her brogue "Hello hiney vaght ye deem?" I replied well nothing in particular just looking around. She grabbed my arm and said "Haway home with me for a meal" Not having encountered situation like that before, I'm afraid that I did her an injustice, and misconstrued her intention. I thought "Hello I've heard about your type before," Oh I can't do that, I don't know you," I said, her reply was" Oh come on it's alright," so off we went.

Later sitting at the meal table chatting with her parents, they told me that they often took in lonely looking soldiers for a meal as part of their war effort. Well, I felt awful and apologized for the injustice that I had done her in thinking that she had another reason for picking me up, as such things were not done in my part of the world. They all laughed at this, after all they had the right idea and it was to our shame that we didn't do similar things at home. I was mortified to learn that they thought that the Isle of Wight was one of the Channel Islands, when they said that they supposed that the Germans were digging up our potatoes to feed their army, I laughingly said that they would have to get past the Home Guard first. I took her to the pictures that night and in the blackout we lost each other in the queue and she shouted "Where yer at?" I replied that I was wearing my hat, but of course I knew that she meant "Where are you?" Although it was April when we were at Spennymore, it was bitterly cold and often snowing and I was glad to get south again.

The next part of the course was at Coventry to Lord Nuffields factories to study the manufacture of Bofors guns and to learn the names of their different parts and how to assemble them. We were based at a heavy Ack-Ack battery just outside of the town, which was manned by downgraded men and ATS girls, I had never been in a mixed camp before and was amazed to find girls manning guns Owing to this fact I nearly got put on a charge for being out of bounds. I was passing a rest room where some ATS girls were playing a record player, Bing Crosby was crooning and I walked in and sat down to listen, when there came a tapping on the window and an irate sergeant major was beckoning me out. Out I went and stood to attention while he tore me off a strip for being out of bounds, I didn't know that I was, but it was useless to plead ignorance, so while he was expounding hot air, my brain was working overtime and being eventually asked what I had to say for myself, I explained that I was passing by and the girls seeing the hammer and tongs had called me in to fix the radiogram that had developed a slight fault, I had just fixed it and was testing it out. He said is that a fact? and I boldly said if you don't believe me ask thegirls. He swallowed my story hook line and sinker and actually apologized, I walked away shocked at my own lucidity, a sergeant major had actually apologized to me and I was in the wrong all the time, they must be slightly human after all.

Our next stop was Newcastle Under Lyme and shortly after we left Coventry it was subjected to a horrific bombing which almost destroyed the city centre and I wondered how the young girl gunners had fared in all that action.

On arrival at Newcastle in the Potteries to learn about heavy Ack-Ack guns and their carriages, we were billeted in a big empty house. Sleeping, as usual on the floor. The weather had been very cold and the previous occupants had burned every piece of wood that they could find in order to keep warm such as the banisters from the stairs, even doors and drawers.

Predictor, Height Finder and a 3.7" Anti-Aircraft Gun

Binley Battery, Coventry

Wedding Day 27th July 1946

Wedding day
27th July 1946

Posing with
Gwen and
Barry on
Brother in
Law Ray's,
Royal Enfield

I Meet Gwen

On our first evening there my mate and I wandered into town to have a look around and perhaps meet a girl. We were going through the park and by this time it was quite dark, when we met and chatted up two very nice young ladies, so we paired up and asked each other's names etc. the girl that I was with was named Gwen. She was nice to talk to and despite the blackout I could tell that she was smartly dressed and good looking. We got along fine but when the time came to take her home, I couldn't afford the bus fare and as it was too far for us to walk. We parted and she caught the bus home alone. We had made a date for the following evening at eight o'clock under the town hall clock, after which we met regularly and I was smitten and very much in love. The Potteries weren't the prettiest of places, but to me it was paradise (Just to be on the street where you live) as the song goes. I'm afraid that I lost all interest in the course and try as I may I just couldn't concentrate and when they told us that if we failed that we could come back again for another try, I resolved to do just that. There was promotion to sergeant if we passed but I just didn't care, all that I could think about was being with her. My head was in the clouds. I was in love. We eventually moved to a barracks which was about six miles from her house, but in order to spend a few more minutes together, we would watch the last bus leave and then I would walk back to barracks, arriving back after lights out every time was very risky I couldn't go through the main gate past the guard, instead I would creep through a hole in the fence at the back of the building. We were sleeping in double tier bunks, mine being the top one and I would make up a dummy, by putting a kit bag under the blankets to give the impression of a sleeping body. The chap in the bunk below knew what was going on and would chuckle at some of the narrow escapes that I had. On Friday afternoons, we used to march to a coalmine pit head for a bath. They called the roll before we left the barracks and again when we returned. We had to march up a steep hill to get to the pithead and the buses going Gwen's way would crawl slowly past us, going up the hill, all that I had to do was ensure that I was right hand man rear rank, enabling me to simply step onto a bus as it slowly passed, the buses had no doors and you paid the conductor, not the driver, as we do today. I had to run up the stairs so as not to be seen through the windows and used to do this every Friday and arrive at Gwen's house with my washing gear under my arm. My mate would answer my name at the roll call when they returned and it worked every time. I didn't mind what risks I ran, I was in love and it was all worthwhile, as well as giving that extra thrill to living. The long walk back to barracks each evening, just didn't register, I was walking on air, ammo' boots and all. It was spring time and the birds were singing even in the Potteries. Could there still be a war on? I wasn't bothered, nothing mattered any more, I feel sorry for anyone who has never experienced that wonderful buzz and feeling of exaltation, it remains in your memory always, no matter what other dreary things may happen, I just think back to those heady days when I was young and in love. That feeling carried me through many trials and tribulations that were to follow.

Having finished the course, I was posted to Tenby in south Wales as a limber gunner and it was there that I witnessed a very traumatic fatality. There were all types of guns here in this training camp, including a prototype of a single barrelled rocket projector, this was in its simplest form as rocket projectors were very much in the experimental stage, there was a class out in the field gathered round a rocket launcher, which simply consisted of two parallel metal rails on a stand, they could be elevated and depressed, or traversed left or right. The rocket itself was about three feet, roughly a meter long and six inches "15 centimetres" in circumference, with a warhead on one end and 4 fins on the other, it was simply laid on the rails with the fins touching two electrical contacts, positive and negative, to fire it you pressed a button which made the electrical contact and away it flew with a roaring noise. There were no shields for the crew.

On this occasion there was a miss-fire, nothing happened when the button was pressed. The instructor carried out the correct drill, which was to wait a certain length of time and then remove the dud rocket. One of the pupils was detailed to go forward and do this, but as he did so there was an explosion which blew him to bits before our eyes. They were very vicious things and shields were then fitted to protect the firing number. In fact, they were soon so successful eventually that they were built to fire 24 rockets at a time.

This particular camp on the cliff at Manorbear, was near to Tenby, a pretty seaside town. From there I was sent to a firing camp for two weeks on the cliffs of Whitehaven Cumberland, here we fired at drogues towed behind aeroplanes, we were in radio contact with the pilots and although this was great fun for us, some of their comments weren't very complementary, especially when the shells were exploding too close to them for comfort, they would say "Hey I'm pulling this B!! !!! thing, not pushing it!" There was also an automatic unmanned target plane known as a Queen Bee which was very expensive and we had to shoot to a given error so as not to shoot it down. This was working fine until the Americans arrived they shot it down with their first shot and thought that they had done something clever.

From there I landed up in St Austell Cornwall for a while on a gun site and then on down to the Lizard, near Lands End. Here we were protecting a huge aerodrome called Predanic. There were all sorts of aircraft on this 'drome which was so large that when the sea mists came rolling in, it was easy to get lost on it.

I wrote regularly to Gwen and spent my leaves with her whenever I could. My older sister Elsie was married before I was posted off of the Island, so that I was able to attend the wedding, now we had the joyful news that she was expecting a baby soon. Her husband Norman was in the infantry, The Royal Wiltshire regiment.

Elsie Died

One Sunday when I was on leave at Gwen's home, we were sitting round the fire talking, when I experienced a dreadful feeling of foreboding, such as I had never felt before and didn't know how to account for it I was in such a state that I couldn't hide it and everyone wanted to know what was wrong, but I couldn't tell them; not knowing myself, but the next morning a telegram arrived saying "Come home immediately, Elsie dangerously ill". I made preparations to go, but Gwen insisted that she would come with me. I explained that she wouldn't be allowed to cross to the Island, as there were strict regulations in force forbidding anyone to land without a special pass, or permit. However, she was adamant that she was going, so I contacted the police chief at Stoke city to try and obtain a permit only to be told that it was at the discretion of the Island police as to whether she could land or not.

This was a most unsatisfactory state of affairs; as imagine how I would have felt if I had to leave her on the other side stranded. So we worried all the way down on the train to Portsmouth, where on showing my pass we were pounced on by the military police, I explained the circumstances and showed them the telegram but they were adamant, saying" You can go but she can't! "Oh yes she can I argued sure of my facts, it is up to the Island police as to if she can land or not and damn all to do with you lot!" where upon they sent an escort of two "Red Caps" with us to make sure that she didn't land without permission from the local police. As luck would have it I knew the Copper on duty on the pier and raced up the gangway saying

"For God's sake get those so and so's off our backs! They won't let my girlfriend land.' He said "Don't take any notice of them tell her to come on, I'm sorry to hear that your sister died." Well! I could have fallen off of the pier, because I didn't know that she had died, tragically in childbirth at the very time that I had that awful feeling at Gwen's home.

After the funeral we travelled back together, there were no restrictions on leaving the Island. I have had no regard for the Red Caps before or since and never met a soldier yet who had a good word for them.

Posted Overseas

Then in January 1943 it happened as I knew it must sooner or later, a posting overseas. I was granted two weeks' embarkation leave, known to the troops as (embrocation) leave and then had to report to Woolwich Arsenal barracks in London. First I went to Gwen's home for a week and then we travelled down together to the Island. The days passed pleasantly enough until Thursday the 4th of February when we were strolling along the beach at Appley near Ryde, it was mid-day the tide was out and we were out on the sands, suddenly the air raid sirens started on the town we heard some bombs going off and found ourselves being machine gunned by a German fighter bomber as it headed out to sea. Luckily we weren't hit, we could clearly see the pilot looking down at us as he passed over us and all that I could do was to shake my fist at him. Gwen was shaken up of course and I laughed foolishly and said that I was used to being shot at. She reproached me for laughing and said that although we were all right, some poor souls had just been bombed, with this sobering thought we hurried homewards.

On the way I asked a chap, that I knew, where the bombs had dropped, he hesitated as he said "I'm afraid that they are up your way" I left Gwen and ran the rest of the way, as I approached our street, there was a crowd gathered on the corner and the police had cordoned the road off I roughly fought my way through the crowd and could see the wreckage where our houses should have been. A policeman tried to stop me and in my agitation I made to strike him shouting that I lived there, he quickly let me through. Thank God my mother and father were safe, although they were badly shaken up. They had heard the bomb screaming down and Dad pushed Mum under the big deal kitchen table and dashed under the stairs, this saved their lives, but some of the neighbours weren't so lucky. My uncle

George was in the house with them and had been in the toilet at the time, fortunately he too was uninjured, but he never lived it down that Hitler had caught him with his trousers down, some crudely joked that he had been constipated before the raid, but wasn't afterwards. At such a time as this, material things don't matter, the great thing was that they were alive and we were very grateful for that. Dad's brother uncle Bill lived not far away and he took us all in with him for the time being.

I was due back the next day and hated the thought of leaving them in such a plight, but the police contacted the army for me and I was granted another two days leave. When the day came that we had to go, Gwen and I realizing that we would be parted for a long time, decided to get engaged, we bought the ring on the way to the ferry, I saw her off on the train at Euston station and waved goodbye until she was out of sight, I was not to see her again for three long years.

I had to report to Woolwich Arsenal barracks in London and as usual got talking to the chap in the next bed to me. We had been granted two days off and I decided to visit my relatives in Wandsworth, but I was broke as usual and casually asked this chap if he could lend me half a crown = 2 shillings and 6 pence roughly 12p. He said what collateral have you got? I didn't have a clue what he was talking about never having been asked that question before and said what do you mean? He said you have a nice watch there, I'll take that as collateral, at that I became very angry and told him what to do with his half a crown in no uncertain terms. It turned out that he was a Jew and there were 6 of them in our draft. This fact meant nothing to me and I borrowed the money from another mate and no questions asked as we trusted each other and off I went to Wandsworth.

They were delighted to see me, it turned out that they were communists and were going to a meeting that night, so of course I went along with them. Germany was attacking the Russians at that time and the people at the meeting were running down our Prime Minister Churchill and calling for a second front to take the pressure off of the Russians. I looked all around the hall and thought well if we do have a second front, who is going to go? I was the only one in uniform! All the protesters were civilians, although Tom and Alan my cousins who I was with, both joined the Royal Navy later.

I stayed the night and had to return in the morning but to my dismay there was a heavy fog and no buses running. There was no underground station at Wandsworth, the nearest one was The Oval I think it was and that was a bus ride away, there was nothing for it but to walk, but I had to find my way, not easy in a fog in a strange place. I kept asking the way but few people could help, any way I eventually made it, but it was a nightmare journey. I reported back to barracks and with secrecy being paramount, we had no idea where we were going to be sent although rumour was rife.

We were marched through London one day to the Quartermasters stores, to collect tropical kit; this made us think that we were heading for the Middle East. There was the usual chaffing and mickey taking as we tried on our kit and some of the sights were comical I must admit, it fitted where it touched so that ribald remarks such as "Are they long shorts or short longs?" and "Doctor Livingstone I presume" were flying about, but by swapping and changing we managed to get some sort of a fit.

The Jewish chap said to me we won't go abroad you know, I said don't be daft, that is what we are here for. No I don't mean you lot he said I mean us 6 Jews, I said how do you make that out then? You are in the draft the same as everyone else. He said the Rabbi will get us off you wait and see. I thought no more about it until we formed up on the square to march off and the order came "Fall out these 6 men." and sure enough all 6 of them fell out and watched us march away. I have never understood that, and never will, if we had been going to Europe against the Germans, yes that would have been understandable in case they were captured, but we weren't so what was the reason?

We entrained to Liverpool docks. The troop train stopped at the dock side and we formed up on the platform our white kit bags on our shoulders, we were marched off in single file towards a great steel wall with port holes, as we moved along we were divided into sections, each section being allotted a mess deck by letters, ours was H deck which turned out to be 8 decks down and right forward in the bows. I remarked to my mate that I didn't much care for that position right up in the bows for I knew that we were in for a bumpy ride when the ship started rolling and pitching. We told each other that when the going got rough, we would go topsides amidships like we used to do on the steamers at home. Some hopes!! A. B. and C. decks were out of bounds and reserved for Officers and nurses only. Typical! We thought disgustedly.

On first inspection our new home looked spacious enough; it was a large room with long tables and benches bolted to the floor. Did I say spacious? It was until we all crowded into it we then had the problem of where we were going to sleep, overhead there were rows of hammock hooks, my mate and I quickly grabbed a hammock each. There were not enough to go round and so chaps had to sleep on and under the tables and in any corner they could find.. We stowed our kits and then went on deck to watch the loading. From our elevated position on the rail, we looked down on the long lines of troops, hundreds of them still coming aboard with their white kit bags on their shoulders they looked like long strings of sausages coming up the gangways, there was much hustle and bustle as the dockside cranes worked busily loading stores.

It seemed that there were standing orders on every baulk head, full of does and don'ts, and we had to wear life jackets day and night while at sea. We got organised after a fashion and settled down as soldiers do.
Eventually the engines started humming and we knew that it wouldn't be long before we were on our way. There would be no waving fond farewells to our dear homeland, which many would never see again, because the good ship Strathmoor sailed at night. It was February 1943 and bitterly cold.

Reveille was sounded on the ships tannoy system, and there was a mad scramble to get up and square away the hammocks and bedding ready for ablutions and breakfast. To our surprise the ship was stationary again; apparently we were standing by, waiting to take up our position in the gathering convoy of ships. Looking through the portholes we could see other ships forming up in line, with the naval escort vessels fussing round them, like sheep dogs herding their charges into position.

At last we got underway, the Irish Sea was very rough making the land lubbers feel queasy and as I had anticipated because we were in the bows we were rising up as in a lift, and crashing down again with a shuddering jar. With this stomach churning motion, it wasn't long before the boys were feeling really sea sick. I put my head out of the porthole for some fresh air and looked aft there was a head out of every porthole with their mouths wide open vomiting. We were heading north and then west round the top of Ireland, the conditions got even worse and the sailors came round and closed and locked the portholes. The lads were fainting or lying on the floor praying for death. The atmosphere was atrocious, but we had to stick it out. After a few days we began to get our sea legs and cheer up again.
The food was good and plentiful; we had fresh baked bread and a well-

stocked canteen. Lifeboat drill was taken very seriously, we were lucky and had a lifeboat allocated to us, many didn't and in the event of having to abandon ship could only hope that they got to a life raft.

Volunteers were called for to do cleaning work I was given the job with some others of cleaning and polishing the main stairway every day, this helped to pass the time away. We had several alarms which caused some excitement, but fortunately we were not attacked although at times we heard distant gunfire and knew that the navy were doing their stuff on our behalf. As we neared the tropics, we changed into our khaki drill and of course all the old jokes came trotting out again and time passed until one morning we awoke to great excitement we were anchored in a large estuary with palm trees and emerald green hills, word went round that this was Africa.

Africa

We were in Freetown on the Gold Coast of Africa. We were there to take on fuel and supplies. The ship was surrounded by native canoes and trader's boats of all kinds known as "Bum Boats" and they were selling fruit and novelties. They would throw a long thin rope up to us on deck and then we could haul up a basket containing our order and the money was sent back down in the basket, meanwhile other natives were diving for sixpenny pieces otherwise known as a tanner and some of the lads would wrap a farthing in silver paper and throw it over and when a diver found one he would shout "You white bastard, a Glasgow tanner!" this would cause roars of laughter and more tanners would be thrown.

Occasionally an unwary canoe would drift under the garbage chutes and get swamped with rubbish, this too caused much laughter and cheeky remarks which the natives seemed to enjoy as much as we did.

While we were at anchor the air conditioning wasn't working and it was very hot, but now we were allowed to sleep on deck, but "A" deck was still out of bounds. It was quite pleasant sleeping on deck but we had to be quick in the morning, the Lascar (Indian) sailors would delight in shouting "Wakey wakey swaby decky!" and before you had a chance to get out of the way they would turn on their hoses dousing you with water, it didn't matter, it gave us and them something to laugh about.

Three days later we again sailed at night and awoke to a beautiful bright morning, I took a stroll along the deck to the after rail and chatted to an old seaman who was leaning on the rail smoking his pipe, after a while he casually asked who had died aboard? I replied that I hadn't heard of any one dying on board, neither have I said he and I thought this is a strange conversation, so I asked him what he was talking about, he said look over there pointing over the rail at the ships wake and there was a shark's fin following us, he said the shark knows that there is a corpse aboard and it will follow us until we ditch it. Sure enough word got round that an Airman had died in the sick bay. He was buried at sea that night without any fuss and the shark had gone in the morning. Conditions were more pleasant now as we sat in the sun playing Bingo or "Housey Housey" as it was called then and had impromptu concerts. Chaps would get up a concert party to entertain us, as each one did his turn, he would receive tremendous applause and back chat, it didn't matter if he had any talent or not as each act was loudly cheered anyway! Most evenings we would sit around singing popular songs the most appropriate being Red sails in the sunset and some of Vera Lynn's sentimental songs.

Our boat drills now were routine, but we had other forms of training such as physical jerks, and unarmed combat was led by a young Captain, who would have us sitting round him in a circle, He would call out a victim and having demonstrated the hand holds proceed to throw the man over his shoulder etc. He seemed to pick on the big built quiet types, but he did it once too often, he beckoned out one young man who was sitting there minding his own business, saying that he wasn't paying attention. The chap just stood there looking at the instructor who said "Well you have just been shown that move, come on attack me" the next thing that the instructor knew, he was on his back with a bang and held in a strangle hold. He slapped the deck in submission and on getting up asked the chap if he would like to be his assistant, as he obviously knew his stuff, we of course were tickled to see the cocky so and so get his comeuppance!

The days passed with no sight of land and then we saw in the far distance a mountain with a flat top, it was the famous Table Mountain of South Africa. We sailed on and watched it disappear over the horizon. Still we had no idea where we would end up, the secrecy was necessary, so that had we been shipwrecked and captured we couldn't tell the enemy where we were going. We knew enough geography to realize that we had rounded the Cape of Good Hope and passed from the Atlantic to the Indian Ocean and there was much speculation as to our next port of call, would it be Durban we wondered?

In the absence of any maps, we had to rely on our knowledge of geography to try and guess the next port and then again would we stop when we got there? It was all speculation and rumour, but sure enough it was Durban and at last we were allowed to go ashore, but slept on board.
It was my bad luck to be detailed for gangway guard, so I couldn't go ashore until later than the others. This was a pity because the good people of Durban had been collecting chaps from the boat and taking them to their homes. Coming from austere war torn Briton with its black out, rationing and general shortages, Durban seemed to be a veritable fairy land of plenty. Goods were very cheap with food, fruit and drinks of all kinds. Brandy was only sixpence a glass and some chaps were sick with over indulgence.

This was a modem thriving city, one of the novelties of which, was the rickshaws, pulled by huge Zulu like natives who wore colourful headdress of ostrich feathers and large cow or buffalo horns on the sides of their heads, the troops made sport with them, with back chat and laughter, they would run along and suddenly jump high in the air causing the rickshaw to tip right back to frighten the occupant! It wasn't unusual to see a rickshaw going by, being pulled by one of our chaps and the rickshaw boy sifting in the back laughing and shouting just for the fun of it. We were there for three days and on one occasion, three of us were walking in the suburbs, when we were passing a bungalow with the occupants sitting on the veranda and they called us in for a meal and when we were introducing ourselves they were quite pleased to hear that my name was Kemp, they informed me that it was a Dutch name and that my ancestors must have been Dutch like theirs. They informed us that we were bound for India and when we asked how they could possibly know that they laughed and said that we would discover that it was true, but you don't need to go they said, stay with us and we will find you a job up country no questions asked. We all indignantly declined the offer as unthinkable. We later learned as we prepared to sail, that not all of us had had such scruples. When the roll was called there were three men missing, one of them was named Smart and you can imagine the comments whenever that name was called until we sailed. On we travelled for week after week, until we were sailing up the Red sea, and a little cockney chap remarked that it would be a fine thing if the Red sea should open up now! Wouldn't it? This caused a laugh as we hadn't thought of the matter until then. On the way up the Suez Canal, the desert was so close that the Arabs with their camels were within hailing distance at times and boats passing certainly were, so if we passed a troop ship there were shouts of "Hey you are going the wrong way!" etc. At Port Said we unloaded troops and airmen for the Middle East, but were not allowed ashore. We then returned down to Aden for refuelling, the heat was stifling, as we were not yet fully acclimatized, and we could understand why the old soldiers always referred to it with dread, whenever the barren rocks were mentioned, as it was known as a punishment station.

There was more room aboard now that we had parted with some of our comrades and more freedom of movement, although the top decks were still out of bounds.

It was difficult to keep out of the sun, because you could fall asleep in a nice shady spot, only to wake up sweating profusely, because the ship had altered course and you were in the sun again. On the final stage of our journey across to Bombay, the sea which sparkled like diamonds was so clear that the screw of a passing ship could be seen through the water. The sun bore down each day glistening off of the flying fish shoals of which skimmed away from our bows, they would fly for quite a long distance before re-entering the water, they were fascinating to watch. At night the moonlight on the water was beautiful and the ships wake was aflame with phosphorescence. The whole thing would have been very romantic if only we had been in the right company.

India

When at last we reached Bombay we had been on that ship for an incredible three months, but now we wished that we could turn around and go right back again. It was a great adventure, but there was much more to come and it would be three long years before I would see England again. By sea it took months for our mail to get home, until we were able to use air mail. We came alongside and made fast amid the hustle and bustle of that busy port, the engines were stopped and we were assembled on deck for a lecture on "Hygiene in the tropics" basically the lecture was about the evils of brothels, which were out of bounds to us anyway. We were reminded of the fact that VD or venereal disease was considered a self-inflicted injury and any soldier who was rash enough to get infected had to pay for his own treatment. A single man had his pay cut, but a married man had his marriage allowance cut and his wife was made aware of the reason. The trouble is that they stupidly went on to tell us where the out of bounds brothels were, so that we were told to keep away from the Grant Road area.

Unfortunately there are always the hot headed types who think that they can beat the system and delights in going against authority and take risks, as soon as they were allowed ashore some of them jumped into rickshaws and headed for Grant road, luckily these types are few and have to learn the hard way, like we had to do with the beggars, these maimed and pitiful creatures crowded round us knowing that we were a soft touch and we gave away all our loose change, the old campaigners laughed at us, "You will learn that you can't keep that up." they said and we found that we had to harden our hearts and ignore them, not an easy thing to do, they are very persistent, waving their out stretched palm and crying "Baksheesh" meaning Alms. The old joke is that is why India is called the land of the waving palm!

We slept aboard for a day or too while batches of us were sent off to different Units needing reinforcements, in all parts of the country. When our turn came we were issued with enough rations for several days and marched to the station. We boarded a train to a place called Ranchi in the central provinces, hundreds of miles across to the centre of the continent. Rail travel in India has to be seen to be believed! The platforms are crowded to capacity with chattering people, vendors and beggars are calling their wares. Some of the beggars are deliberately physically deformed to promote sympathy; they are covered in flies which come from them on to you.

 Dhoti (a white cloth worn between the legs and around the waist) clad porters with little pads on their heads, for carrying loads on their heads, as soon as someone arrives with a package, suit case, or kitbag, they grab it, as competition is fierce and trot off through the bustling crowd to the train and wait for you to catch up, to give them a small "Baksheesh" as a tip is called. The first time that you experience this, you think "Hey! He has pinched my kitbag!" and you dash after him desperately trying to keep your eye on your precious kit as it progresses along over the heads of the teaming crowd, but you soon get used to it.

In all this seething humanity there are people moving along the platform selling sweetmeats and fit-bits to eat, these are ignored because of the flies, which are impossible to avoid, as there are so many of them. We were warned of course not to drink any untreated water, but there were "Char-

Wallas" or tea sellers, with their portable tea making gear, from whom it was considered safe to buy tea. Ours were reserved third class coaches, with wooden seats, with our luggage in the rack overhead. The toilets were a joke to us until we tried to use them, it was simply a hole in the floor with two grab rails and when the train was travelling fast and swaying about as they do, it was very uncomfortable to say the least.

Our rations consisted mainly of "Bully Beef and Biscuits" the biscuits were what's known as "hard tack" and they were so hard that you couldn't bite them, they had to be soaked first, and they were always full of dead weevils, the lads used to reckon that they were extra protein!

As soon as the train stopped for any reason, two of us would run up to the engine carrying a large dixie and call out to the driver for "garam pani" or hot water, he would pull a lever and boiling water for making tea would squirt from a pipe connected to the boiler into our dixie.

The countryside varied considerably, sometimes it was lush and green with rice paddy fields, here you might see a native using a wooden plough pulled by bullocks just as they did in biblical times, but mostly it was dry dusty plain and you wondered what they lived on, it varied a lot, according to the seasons and the answer is of course that the rice and cereals are grown in the rainy season and stored for use during the dry season.

The unit that we were joining as reinforcements was situated in the centre of India and so we were on the train for about a week, stopping in sidings sometimes at night, to get some sleep. In the early morning when passing a village in the distance, it was interesting to see the villagers trekking off out into the countryside for their toilet, as they have no lavatories at home. Each person carries a small brass pot called a "Peala", to wash themselves instead of toilet paper. They always use their left hand only for this purpose and as they don't use eating utensils, such as a knife fork spoon, or even chopsticks, they use their right hand only to roll their rice balls with spices added and perhaps millet and other cereals. They pick it up with their fingers from a dish on the floor, while squatted on their haunches and all picking from the same dish while trying to ignore or brush away the flies at the same time while starving mangy looking dogs slink about with their tails between their legs, hoping for a titbit.

The railways have been run traditionally by Anglo Indians for generations and they really know their business. The travelling public always over crowd a train and will squeeze in where ever they can, with scant regard for comfort, or safety, I have seen them on the buffers and in all kinds of odd places, one train that we were on stopped suddenly because a native who had been clinging on to the hand rails outside of the door, had been struck by an obstacle that we were passing, which killed him and someone had pulled the communication cord. There was no sleeping accommodation on the train, we simply made ourselves as comfortable as we could on the hard wooden seats, some sleeping up in the racks, to awake stiff and bleary eyed in the morning. The trains seemed to trundle on forevermore, but then India is a vast continent and extremely hot.

The paddy fields are man-made terraces on the hillsides surrounded by low walls made of raised earth called Bunds to conserve the water and ploughed by those primitive wooden ploughs pulled by one or sometimes two oxen, it was strange to us that such primitive methods were still in use, the young rice plants are then planted by hand. Occasionally there are wells and the water is raised by the use of a simple crane consisting of a long wooden pole pivoted in the centre to an upright stake, there is a rope and leather bucket on the longest end of the pole and a large stone as a counter balance lashed onto the other end, this is raised to allow the bucket to descend into the well and lowered again to raise the water up, it is then tipped into an irrigation canal, slow and laborious work.

All this was weird and wonderful to us being newcomers and the magnificent sunsets with the black silhouettes of the tall coconut palms against the crimson sky was all very exotic to us. Such scenes of course were soon to become part of our everyday environment and were soon taken for granted. The old soldiers that we encountered along the way would pull our legs with chit chat such as "Who is on the throne of England now then?" And so on. We had no idea what lay ahead of us in the future, which was just as well and at the moment we were content to let the future take care of itself.

Our New Unit

When we finally detrained at Ranchi in the province of Chota Nagpir, we transferred to lorries and proceeded to our new Unit which was the 44th Light Ack-Ack Regiment, 33 India Corps. They had just seen some action in the Arakan against the Japanese and had returned to India to recuperate.

This was a tented camp in what I can only call semi desert, the earth was sandy with specks of Formica glistening in the sun, with huge granite rocks here and there and the vegetation was sparse thorny shrubs, with an occasional stunted tree and the heat was extreme.

We were well received by the lad's eager for any news of conditions at home, late though the news was. Our cork topees (hats) were handed in and replaced with Bush Hats so that we looked more like soldiers and less like Victorian Missionaries we still wore KD or khaki drill, comprising of a bush shirt, shorts, knee socks, canvas gaiters ammo' boots and webbing belt and equipment, all the webbing was blancoed green of coarse, including belt and gaiters and brass and boots were still highly polished there was no slackening of standards!

Our new comrades having seen some action, had many stories to tell and much advice to give us about jungle warfare and how to exist in this strange country, there was the usual chaff like "You wanna get yer knees brown."
They had received some casualties mainly through disease and were glad to see us. Some were suffering with dysentery and jungle sores. These sores are ulcers and would eat right through to the bone if not properly treated, they were caused we were told, by leeches being knocked off, the best way was to touch them with a burning cigarette end, or wait until they had their fill and dropped off naturally. If you by instinct knocked the repulsive thing off, they left their head under the skin and caused the ulcer, this was just one of the things that they warned us about.. We were advised to always turn our boots upside down and tap them out in the morning before putting them on, in case there may be a scorpion in them, this was no leg pull, but "puka gen'" or straight talk, as we found out. Such things as scorpions, large multi-coloured centipedes and spiders were common place. We had to wear long sleeves and slacks from sunset onwards by order, as protection against the dreaded malaria mosquitoes.

Our beds consisted of a rough wooden frame on legs crisscrossed with cord, such as the natives used, called a "charpoy", we had mosquito nets, but when we let them down to tuck them in round the bed, we always had to use a torch to kill the bed bugs advancing on us from above, as we squashed them they had a revolting smell. The termite ants could eat the bottom out of a kit bag over night and we were constantly brushing them off of the guy ropes. It was an offence to allow them to attack the guy ropes so a tent orderly was detailed daily for this task. There were some birds similar to a kestrel called kite hawks although that isn't the only thing that we called them! They were magnificent flyers, as good if not better than a seagull and they would line up on the cookhouse roof and swoop down on the unwary as you emerged with your dixie, or tin plate and knock it right out of your hand on to the floor and pick up the food all in one movement. If you were unfortunate enough to be caught out, it caused much merriment and catcalls. The trick was to crisscross your arms across your chest so that the food was under your arms, if you didn't do this you would be caught out every time. It was so hot that the sweat patches on the back and front of our shirts dried white with salt, and there was a salt tablet issued to every man on parade each morning, which had to be swallowed there and then, to make sure that it had been taken. Practically all of the chaps were afflicted with a mild skin disease of some sort, mainly prickly heat which takes the form of being covered in tiny blisters which itch, this condition we called "Dhoby itch"!

The Gecko lizards were comical to watch, being able to change their colour to match their surroundings, they were harmless and helped to keep the flies down but some of the other many types of insects we tried to ignore, the scorpions, large spiders and centipedes weren't welcome and were exterminated by a size 9 boot. There were vicious flying insects as well.
I became friendly with a chap in the same tent as me named Fred, and we got along very well.

Wireless Course

There came an opportunity for a Driver Wireless Operators course and we both applied for it, and were accepted. This was a lengthy course involving learning the Morse code, operating a wireless, learning wireless procedure, charging batteries and driving.

I suppose that it lasted about a month before we passed out. One chap couldn't get on with it because he was a pianist and the rhythm of the Morse sent him off on a tune and he couldn't concentrate and had to give it up. We had to learn to drive on a big Matador gun tractor, under a crazy American from New York who had joined the British army, he was a right "Nut Case" and everything was a huge joke to him. We all piled in the back and set off to take turns at learning to drive this big lorry. For some unknown reason he took us along a narrow track which twisted and turned up the steep side of a mountain, with a sheer drop down one side, he probably did it on purpose to put the wind up us, because that is the sort of thing that he would do. Most of the chaps had some experience, but I didn't have a clue, never having had the chance to learn before and this was my big opportunity. Anyway when it came my turn we were on the way down again, so I got in behind the wheel and said "Before we start Yank, how do I stop?" I was serious but this was a big joke to him and he roared with laughter thinking that I was having him on and I couldn't convince him otherwise, don't kid me he kept saying you can drive. So we started rolling down this very steep hill, I was terrified and trying not to show it and every time I said how do I slow down? Or where is the brake? he laughed all the more, until coming round a bend we were confronted with a drover coming up with a small herd of cows, I simply weaved in and out through the cattle and on coming out the other side I glanced at the Yank who had his hands over his eyes, saying "Holy Mackerel! you've convinced me" and he wasn't laughing any more, I reckon that he was just as scared as I was.

That course was very interesting and they were a good bunch of mates. Fred came from Stockport and was courting a girl named Alice and I told him about Gwen and we used to compare notes from then on looking forward to a letter and chatting about the things that we used to do, we were special mates and kept together whenever we could and later on we had many adventures together. We kept in touch even when we were apart I knew his touch on the Morse key and strictly against regulations would send (dit dit dadit dit da dit da da didy) = Fred. He would reply (dit dit dit dit dit dit dit da dit dit da) = Hilt. We still kept in touch after the war for 50 years until Alice informed me that he had died after a stroke.

One day we were issued with leather belts and ammunition pouches, which were covered in preservative grease and given orders to wash them in hot water to remove the grease. So we heated some water in a dixie over a fire and got on with the job successfully, but there is always one dozy so and so! And when it came to inspection time he produced what I can only describe as a hand full of chitterlings, he had boiled his until they had all shrivelled up. I expect that he had to pay for them, as that was the practice if any kit was lost or damaged, it was stopped out of our measly pay. This was known as Barrack room damages. Consequently, on kit inspections there was quite a bit of wangling going on. The drill was for all kit to be laid out on the bed correctly according to a drawing on the notice board, prior to the parade being called, each man tells his mates and bed neighbour what items he is short of, they ensure that the first man in line has a full lay out and as the officer is passing on to the next man, any items that he is needing suddenly and mysteriously appears on his bed so that he too has a full layout and so on. It is comical to watch the officer being fooled like this but everyone must keep a straight face and stand at attention by his bed until we are dismissed and then we would have a chuckle about it.

This was a time when the army consisted of all types of men good and bad, but it was very unusual for anyone to steal from his mates, we had one such incident I recall, when chaps kept missing things and reluctantly we had to conclude that we had a thief among us, so one chap volunteered to try and catch him. The one that we suspected was a shifty individual, always playing cards but although he lost quite a bit, always seemed to have plenty of money, so one day when the suspect was tent orderly which meant that he was excused parades, our detective for the purpose went sick and was also excused parades, hid himself under a bed to keep watch, sure enough he caught this thief red handed going through our pockets and kit. Now the question was what to do about it, the obvious thing was to report him to the powers that be, but they decided against that as it would have meant a court marshal and prison so they decided to teach him a lesson instead. They roughly frog marched him down to a nearby swampy pond and with a rope round his middle some were on one side of the pond and some on the other, each with an end of the rope they dragged him backwards and forwards through the stinking mud until he begged for mercy, only then did they let him go and no one would have anything to do with him after that, they sent him to Coventry as it is called and I reckon that is the worst thing of all, it would have been for me I'm sure. This was the only incident of stealing that I encountered throughout my service thank goodness, I never wanted to witness anything like that again.

Training

Gun drills and other training was going on all the time, we now had a proper dining hall come lecture room with a platform at one end, probably for concerts, although we hadn't had any up until now, but there was talk of forming a concert party. One day everyone that could be spared had to attend a lecture in there, this was a big do, with the officers and senior N.C.O's standing at the back. Our section was sitting at the front. A sergeant major "Ack I G" (Antiaircraft instructor gun) was about to give a lecture on the Buffer a device to slow down the recoil on big guns. Our Bofors guns didn't have them, using powerful springs instead, so the lads hadn't come into contact with the Buffer but I had, on the gun fitting course. It is common practice for the instructor to pick on some poor unfortunate chap and claim that he is not paying attention, to make sure that everyone is on their toes and listening.

He stood on the platform leaning on the table giving a preamble about the buffer and its purpose, when suddenly he picked on me saying that I wasn't paying attention, just for that you can come up here and carry on with the lecture. He thought that he was making a mug of me, as we weren't supposed to have come across a buffer before, but he dropped a "clanger," I thought "Right Matey, I'll show you a thing or two! If that's the way you want it,"

I marched up on to the platform and said to the audience, before I start, it is no use me talking to you about something that you cannot see, can I have a blackboard and easel please, the instructor brought it and set it up probably thinking that I was playing for time I thanked him and have you any half section models please, he produced some from a cupboard and set them up on the table, thinking no doubt that I was still stalling for time, I thanked him again very politely and then started my lecture explaining how you cannot compress a liquid therefore oil is used to flow through the venturi and explained what a venturi was, he was so astounded that he was lost for words and forgot to stop me I was in my element and really putting it across, until he recovered and said alright that's enough go and sit down and he carried on with the lecture. Afterwards when we got back to our tents and were sitting on our beds chatting, the battery runner came in and said "Here the colonel wants you" and I said "Pull the other one, push off!" "No I'm not kidding" he said, I have given you the message in front of witnesses and if you don't go I'm not responsible and off he went. When you get a summons like that from on high it usually spells trouble, so I smartened myself up and reported to the battery office and was ushered into the presence of the great one. I saluted smartly and awaited the tirade. The colonel bade me stand at ease with a stern look on his face "Kemp" he said, "you made a right Charlie out of that Ack I G, you shouldn't have done that you know," I replied, "sorry sir but he did pick on me". He asked where I had learned the subject and I told him about the gun fitting course, so he said," well you obviously know your stuff and how to give a lecture, so I am promoting you to lance bombardier acting unpaid dismiss."
I didn't want a stripe, three times I had been made lance bombardier acting unpaid and I knew that you get all the jobs that the other N.C.O's don't like, such as giving the chaps on jankers pack drill on the square night and

morning, believe me on that job you really get told your fortune and your ancestors get insulted as well! No I was quite content to stay as I was with my mates, so I told the sergeant major that I didn't want it and why, and that was that.

Leave in Calcutta

Now having passed out on our Driver Operators course (Dvr' Op') for short, we were granted 7 days leave in Calcutta. We were issued with a pass and travel warrant for the train journey and then asked how much money we needed? This set us back in astonishment never having been asked such a question before, of course we said why how much are we entitled to? Apparently we could have as much as we wanted but it was paid back out of our weekly pay, we didn't spend much in camp as there wasn't much to spend it on, so we thought it a good idea and we drew 500 Rupees each, and on receiving it had never felt so rich before, now we drew rations for a long train journey to the city.

Our bed and board was at a transit camp, but there were no restrictions as to lights out or reporting in or out. This was within walking distance of the city and on our first day Freddy and I had a good meal at "Firpos" a restaurant which was popular with the troops, we ordered a T bone steak and all the trimmings and pudding to follow. This was the best meal that we had eaten for a long time and we called there every day during our leave.

After strolling round the bazaars we decided to go to the cinema called The Light House and joined a long queue in a side street. There were troops there from all parts of the commonwealth and it was quite a large crowd waiting to go in, we were laughing and chatting away, when along came an Indian entertainer or "Cunjeroo" as they are called and said that he would perform a miracle such as we had never seen before if he could collect enough "baksheesh". So he started collecting our donations occasionally stopping to rattle his little drum and play his whistle pipe. When he considered that he had enough money, he called a small boy out of the crowd, and asked him to lie down on the ground, he then unwound a large yellow turban from his head and covered it over the boy. Then he stood back, rattled his drum, played his whistle pipe and prayed to his gods, for good effect. Then he raised his arms and commanded ("Ooper rockko") meaning rise up and the whole thing keeping perfectly rigid rose slowly up to a height of about 4 feet when he commanded (Bus Olgia) meaning stop. He then passed his hands round the body to prove that there were no props supporting it and said ("Neechi rockko") meaning descend and it slowly returned to the ground. Whereupon he took off the turban and the boy got up and walked away.

Well I have seen levitation on the stage since, where props could have been used, but this was in the middle of the road!

As I have remarked before there is always one joker and I expect that he had been on the booze, but this chap starting blaspheming and swearing at this Indian, shouting, "you so and so You have hypnotized us" so the Indian said "you no believe Sahib?" and he drew a circle round this chap's feet in the dust and said "alright Sahib you walk!" The chap struggled and spluttered, but was unable to move his feet, thus causing much merriment and cat-calling among his friends and he was well and truly shown up. In the end he had to apologize and calm down, then the Indian said," alright Sahib you can walk now" and only then was he able to walk away. If I had to describe Calcutta at that time from our point of view, I would say hot, very over- crowded and untidy, but very interesting, though not a place that I would choose for a holiday, still we had no choice, but to make the best of it.

Sad to say there was a terrible famine at that time and it wasn't unusual to see a body lying in the gutter and people stepping over it. We saw 6 coolies trotting along with a grand piano upside down on their heads, through the busy streets teaming with humanity, all doing what they can to make a living, there were rickshaws, bullock carts and horse drawn cabs called "Tongas" the horses just skin and bone.

The bazaars were full of everything that you could think of and the traders called "Wallahs" selling their wares and making things there on the pavements in the blazing sun. We decided to have a new pair of "chappals" each, that is the Hindi word for sandals. They are leather sandals with two wide straps from toe to ankle which cross over each other, one side is fixed and the other ends in a strap for the buckle and just one strap at the back, like an open toed shoe. They are very comfortable and hard wearing, but not bought in a shop, you go along to a cobbler right there on the pavement, take off your shoe and place your foot on a piece of paper, he then draws a line round your foot and likewise for the other one to get the shape of your feet and in a day or two you can collect the finished article quite cheaply.

So it is with the tailor, made out there in the open to your specifications and comfort. Lots of other crafts are carried out there on the pavement, such as copper, brass and tin smiths and weavers of carpets and all kinds of rush and bamboo baskets and furniture, all along the roads doing their stuff. They expect you to bargain, it is all in the game, we would try to knock the price down saying no it's too dear and pretend to walk away, they would run after you saying "Me very poor man, Sahib three wives fifteen children you Rajah!" And we would reply "Don't give us your worries," they would wring their hands and pretend to cry and when the price was agreed on and paid, they would be laughing having got the best of the bargain after all, it was a game with them and they enjoyed it.

We witnessed one very ugly incident, again in a cinema queue one afternoon, we saw three black American service men get out of a taxi, probably having just flown in to India, as they were the first GIs that we had seen, they appeared to be a bit merry and were shouting "Say, we ain't seen no dames around here!" and we thought no you won't either unless you go to a brothel, as the locals jealously guarded their women, but that is by the way.

In this cinema queue there were all nationalities Aussies, Kiwis, Gurkhas, Indians Brits and African troops both East and West African were represented, and these black GIs took their place in the queue directly beside some black Africans, who incidentally had their pangas hanging from their belts. The panga is a big extremely sharp knife used to slash your way through the jungle. The GI's were still very vocal and one of them in particular was making offensive remarks about the black Africans, probably not realizing that they understood English. Making remarks about them being monkeys straight off the trees and things like that and laughing at them, the Africans didn't reply but tried to ignore them, but they kept it up and became even more insulting. Still the Africans said nothing but like a flash one of them drew the panga from its scabbard and all in one motion beheaded the most vocal of them! It was so fast that the first thing that we knew was blood spurting everywhere and a mad scramble to get out of the way. We got out of there fast feeling sick at the whole affair.

The next day we met one of the African white N.C.O's. We knew that he was from the same unit by his shoulder flash, which was I believe a black elephant, so we asked him what would happen to the murderer? He laughed and said don't worry about him, he is a good bloke and he is already on his way up the line out of the way, after all the Yanks asked for it and our lot are hardly civilized. One thing is certain I'll bet that they will stay away from black African troops from now on.

By the way, a black African frightened the life out of me once. I was on the alert as I thought in a trench or fox hole as we called it, guarding a cross trail at night in the jungle of Burma, when a deep bass voice suddenly said "the time Effendi, what is it?" I nearly had a heart attack and said to him "Crumbs why don't you frighten anybody?"

His white teeth flashed in the dark and he replied "Ah you no see me, I see you!" I told him the time and off he went, I'd hate to be a Jap' meeting him one dark night. Which reminds me that if we were standing there in the dark and felt a tickle round the ankles, we froze, that was Johnny Gurkha as we called him, checking to identify friend from foe, if he felt a canvas boot, that belonged to a Jap and he would be silently dispatched with the Kukri the Gurkhas favourite weapon, which was a curved knife, come sword, carried by all Gurkha troops. We would whisper "Thic hi Johnny" and he would go on his way, and you would know that you had just had a narrow escape, saved by your ammo' boots and gaiters.

You may have heard about the burning ghats on the banks of the holy river Ganges, we saw them in action, while the faithful bathed in the river to wash away their sins. The Parsees, "descendants of Persians," have a tall tower like a lighthouse called a tower of silence. This has a metal grid at the top, and the corpse is laid on that for the vultures to pick the bones which fall down through the grid into the tower.

We got used to the sight of the holy Brahmin cows wandering where ever they fancied in the traffic and crowds, being sacred, they could wander where they pleased. We saw the monument of the great mutiny of 1857-1858, and a statue of Queen Victoria, the old soldiers used to teach the natives to say "Queen Victoria bloody good man!!"

Of course we all used to smoke in those days and there was a wholesale tobacco merchant's premises which advertised to send 500 cigarettes to any address, so we went in and ordered some to be sent to ourselves, having paid for them, we forgot all about it. A short time later back at camp, I received a parcel addressed to me from Calcutta and was mystified as to who knew me in Calcutta, until I opened the parcel and felt pretty foolish, it should have been April the first. How dumb can you get? All too soon it seemed the leave was up and we were on our way back to the Unit where all the lads wanted to hear about our adventures, and we at least had something to tell them!

Bengal

Before long we were issued with jungle green cotton uniforms, towels, plate, under-clothes and mug, everything green.

Then came the big exodus we were on the move again this time to Bengal for jungle training. Now we were in bamboo huts called "Bashas" cunningly made by plaiting split bamboo to make the walls, on bare earth with thatched roofs. The windows were open squares with a flap to drop down in the monsoon. We slept on Charpoys with mosquito nets. Now it was more training, this time in infantry work, as well as our usual roles.

One day we were on patrol and advancing along a narrow goat track round the side of a steep hill. The leader raised his right arm, a signal to stop and fade into the undergrowth, but this time instead of silence, there was some talk going on up front and we were invited to come on up. Something strange was happening this was not the correct drill. When we got up to the leader they were gathered in a bunch looking at something, which turned out to be a Holy man sitting cross legged at the side of the track as motionless as a statue, just skin and bones, his hair had grown so long that it was matted on the earth round him and the undergrowth was growing up through it, so how long had he been there? There was no movement of his chest, so was he breathing? He was dressed only in a loincloth and looked as though he was in a trance and had not moved for a long time. There was no sparkle in his eye and he had a fixed stare, not even a flicker of an eyelash and he gave no indication that he knew that we were there. Everyone was concerned and marvelled at this phenomena, saying "is he alive or isn't he?" yet one got the impression that he was, give him a poke with your bayonet they joked, but of course they didn't interfere with him, knowing that weird and wonderful things happen out there beyond our comprehension. There was a begging bowl beside him completely empty; the nearest village was miles away as it was. After some discussion we had to continue our patrol and left him unmolested but with our minds full of questions unanswered, was he in some sort of hypnotic trance? What about wild animals at night? He was at their mercy but had survived so far, or had he? Was he alive? Or What? We shall never know.

Back at the hut there was a terrible smell of sweaty socks and we were very fussy about foot hygiene, everyone was suspecting his neighbour and there were accusations and indignant denials going on and we decided that the only way to settle the matter was to have a foot inspection among ourselves, so every inhabitant of the hut sat round the table on forms, with their bare feet on the table and each person had the opportunity to inspect the feet of anyone else as much as they liked. This caused some merriment but didn't solve the mystery, everyone was exonerated, but the smell remained and in fact was getting worse, until one day they were throwing a ball about and it lodged in the thatch, so they climbed up to retrieve it and found a pair of rolled up socks stinking to high heaven, stuffed into the thatch no doubt by previous occupants.

Our wireless communication was now being used in earnest, keeping in touch with convoys, and distant detachments, patrols etc. in Morse code, I knew Fred's touch on the Morse key and when he came up on the air, I would send Fred and he would send back Hilt' this was strictly against regulations, as we had to stick to the procedure laid down, but we did it constantly and got away with it. That way we knew that although we were miles apart, we were still in action.

One of the potentially most dangerous jobs from our point of view was 0 P, or observation post duty, where a {Drvr' Op} = driver operator and a rifleman accompany an Officer out to observe the enemy positions, and wireless back the map reference giving range and bearing and directing the fall of shot. The worst position on patrol was "tail end Charlie "as the last man was sometimes silently knocked off and then the next one etc., so that one had to be constantly checking to see if the chap behind you is still there, if he isn't, watch out! There is a bogeyman about! This sort of thing was what our training was all about, giving us an idea of what to expect.
Off duty there was not much to do, we had paperback books to read and there was a canteen of sorts, though they didn't stock very much, we used to buy a "char and wad"= tea and bap, or from the Char-walla we could buy a char and egg banjo, what is an egg banjo? A bap sliced through, and a fried egg in the middle, otherwise we would sit around telling yarns of back home, or things like that. I would tell of my experiences on the searchlights and funny things that happened such as Pedlar Palmers car. Didn't I tell you that one? Oh Well here goes, it won't take long. We had a Captain named Palmer and since all Palmers are nicknamed Pedlar, so it was with him. Pedlar a tall rangy sort of chap had a Baby Austin car,, and he used to have to curl up small to get behind the wheel. I was in Headquarters one day at the Quartermasters store, which was right opposite the motor transport garage and workshop, which in turn was right next door to the

Company Office. I was idly gazing out of the window, when I saw Pedlar pull up outside of the garage and go into the company office, then to my amazement, six mechanics doubled smartly out, four of them stood round the car with their backs to it, they bent their knees and together lifted the car while the other two men placed oil drums under the axles so that when lowered down the wheels were just clear of the ground. They then doubled back into the garage.

When Pedlar returned to his car, he curled up behind the wheel started the engine and engaged the clutch. Of course the car didn't move, the wheels were turning but he couldn't see them, he revved up but to no avail, so he switched off and uncurled himself out of the car again and went into the garage, out came the sergeant who had no doubt organised the whole thing, and opened the bonnet and scratched his head, fiddled about a bit with the engine, started her up again, with the same result. He then had a word with Pedlar no doubt saying that it may be some job, so Pedlar went back into the office. Out they doubled and reversed the previous performance, setting the car back down on the road and disappeared back into the garage. They waited quite a while before informing Pedlar that the job was done, and he eventually drove off after no doubt tipping the sergeant. I wonder what they told him that the fault was? That they had changed the half shaft or something I expect. I thought "Well I have seen it all, but I had better forget it".

Now let's get back to the present, it is as hot as hell and as usual everyone is suffering from prickly heat, we sweat so much that our shirts are wet through and have a big patch of white salt stain at the back, front and under the arms. Salt tablets are compulsory, as I have said and have to be swallowed as it is issued to you there and then on parade to ensure that every man takes it, they are quite large and not easy to swallow without a drink of water. Also at the same time, we have to swallow a little yellow tablet for the suppression of malaria called mepacrine, notice that I said suppression, it doesn't prevent you catching it, just keeps you going and eventually turns you yellow. The air is so sultry and everyone is forecasting that the monsoon is on its way, and large clouds were gathering.

The Monsoons

One morning I was shaving in the ablutions as usual, when the next thing that I knew I was recovering consciousness on my bed. There was a big blustering Glaswegian sergeant with us who was all wind and water and he was holding my hand and saying "Poor Laddie, poor wee Laddie!" and the tears were trickling down his face, he obviously thought that I was dead, so I let him suffer a while and then said "What's all the fuss about Jock? I'm not dead yet." "You rotten Bastard!" He shouted, peeved that I had caught him in a weak moment. He had a heart after all. It appears that I had Dengue fever caused by a mosquito bite, which gives you a stiff neck and shoulders, but I soon recovered after treatment with no ill effects.

Our camp was on a hill and we were set to digging storm trenches around the huts to run the water away when it came. We had a clear view all around, over a long distance.

All at once the weather broke with a terrific thunder storm, we could actually smell the rain before it came, and looking out we could see it advancing like a curtain until it reached us and then the heavens opened as they say and we all rushed out naked to stand under this lovely cool water, holding our faces up to it and rubbing our arms and bodies to try to get rid of the prickly heat. The rain was almost continuous from then on, with thunderstorms such as never seen in England. The monsoon lasts for three months, non-stop.

You may think that what I am about to tell you now is a tall story, but it is absolutely true, one day I was sitting using the set with earphones on when a bolt of lightning shot past me so close that it knocked the hand set off of the telephone on the table beside me and was gone. I thought, "Crikey that was near enough!" Those storms had to be experienced to be believed.
Now we were inundated with all kinds of crawling insects, coming into the but for shelter, as they were washed out of their holes in the ground, they weren't welcome and we had a job on our hands dissuading them with the aid of our boots, but they still came in while we were asleep and then there was a frenzy of slaughter in the mornings to get rid of them but it was a losing battle, so we had to live with it, but it was wise to turn your boots upside down, and tap them out before putting them on in case of scorpions etc.

One night though, it wasn't only insects that I had for company! I was on listening watch, in contact with a convoy of lorries, in the wireless hut on my own and reading a book by the light of a smoky paraffin lamp, the rain was pouring outside and there was a cloud of moths which kept flying into the lamp and falling to the floor, I took no notice of this as I was used to it, until I noticed a movement near my feet, it was a large frog catching the moths and eating them. That was alright by me, he was welcome, getting rid of the moths, until I heard a scuffle and there was a rat had the frog by the hind legs and they were struggling across the floor. I wasn't going to stand for this, but just as I was taking off the head 'phones to chase the rat, a snake appeared and grabbed it, the rat squealed and let go of the frog who made his getaway pretty damn quick. I sat perfectly still watching this play of the law of the jungle being enacted right before my eyes, as the snake slowly swallowed the rat, it then slithered off into the dark shadows out of sight, it must have been in the hut all along, unless there was a hole somewhere that we didn't know about, anyway I consoled myself that having had a meal it would probably sleep it off, but it was uncomfortable knowing that it was lurking nearby, the door had been shut and the window shuttered against the rain. I was glad to get out when my duty was over. There was no sign of it next morning though we searched the hut thoroughly and of course I warned the lads about it but no one else experienced that again and frogs weren't encouraged anymore.

The monsoon continued on and off for months until we thought that it would never end, everything was damp and mouldy and we were fed up and wished for the sun to shine again. It has occurred to me that I haven't as yet fully described the monsoon, I haven't mentioned the wind that accompanies the storms, they too were quite frightening and reminded me of the whirlwind that swept through a tented camp that we were in, it was the dry season, and a hot wind was blowing that felt as though someone had just opened an oven door, when suddenly we heard a sound like an express train approaching and on looking out saw this tall spiral of dust rushing towards us, we had no time to do anything but hit the dirt. I lay face down with my hands covering the back of my neck as we had been trained to do in the blitz. It passed over as quickly as it came, but it took us a long time to retrieve everything from a great distance around, as tents and kit were scattered far and wide. Luckily no one was hurt as they may have been had we been in buildings.

We trained hard all through the monsoon season which was a sign of things to come for up until then everything used to close down in the rainy season, even the war I was told, but not anymore, it had been decided that we would fight on whatever the season and so we did come hell or high water we soldiered on.

Concert Party

We had some homemade concerts and the lads did their best to entertain us, it was a good excuse for some of the pretty boys to dress up in women's clothing, and act the fool, I must admit that I never had the pluck, or inclination to have a go myself, but I appreciated those that did, and of course they always had lots of encouragement and back chat from the audience, but now at long last was the real thing. George Formby no less, the Lancastrian singing comedian and his party were coming to give us a show. It was advertised on the notice board and the news caused quite a stir. The concert was to start at a certain time and we queued early to get a good seat. It was the accepted thing that the officers didn't queue, but lines of seats were kept vacant in the front rows for them to saunter in having finished their port wine just as the show was about to start. George Formby must have encountered this sort of thing before, but this time he turned awkward, walking out on to the stage, he said to the audience at large, "Why are these seats empty?" and he was told why in no uncertain terms by an almighty shout from the audience. "Oh no!" said George, "I'm not having that, I want you to all go out and queue again and the officers can take their chance with the rest of you!" Well the lads were dumbfounded but they did as they were bidden and queued back in again but the officers boycotted the show, which was their loss and the lads had the front seats as well, they enjoyed the show very much and of course George was a hero.
It was the custom for the officers to entertain the artists as they were called, not stars as they are today, in their mess, but this time they weren't invited. So they came to our mess and George gave a little speech. He said," I don't give a toss about that lot I'm here today and gone tomorrow, not stuck here with them like you poor so and so's."

We only ever had one other official concert. Gracie Fields was another Lancastrian, and as ever she brought the house down! She had her Italian husband with her and the lads were saying, "Who's that chap then?" They didn't know that she was married let alone to an Italian. We were at war with Italy at the time but that had no bearing on the matter of course. On second thoughts though we may have had a visit from Vera Lynn, but I'm not quite sure about that, we heard her so much on the wireless that I may be mistaken. I know that she did come to Burma entertaining the services. Once or twice we had a mobile cinema come to the camp and the films were shown outside at night. It was very amusing to see the local natives creep up to see the films as of course they hadn't seen any before and if anything frightening came on they would rush away and then creep back again. It must have been a great adventure for them seeing films for the-first time, I wonder what they thought of the love scenes, as they are very shocked about that sort of thing and the women never used to expose their bodies and would even bathe fully clothed in public.

Into Burma

Rumour followed rumour, and there was definitely something stirring. Now it seemed, we were on the move again, as we had done so often before. This time, things were different, all our equipment was coming with us, transferring from lorries to train, we were off on a long journey, so it would seem that the rumours were true we were going into action at long last, and heading for Burma.

Tokyo Rose, Japan's equivalent to Germany's Lord Haw-Haw, was crowing on the wireless that the Japs were poised ready to invade India, they had reached the borders. It was probably our strategy to stretch their lines of communication to the limit, and then drive them back. At Calcutta everyone and everything, had to change to a narrow gauge track, we were running along beside the holy river Ganges at times and saw crowds of people in places where steps came down from the temples, bathing and washing away their sins, the women as usual fully clothed, in the water. Gradually the scenery was changing and becoming more greener and lush, the railhead stopped at the next river which turned out to be the Brahmaputra, and was not bridged. There we embarked on to old paddle steamers, and chugged on up the river watching the changing scenery, and were fascinated to see crocodiles basking along the bank and at times elephants hauling logs, probably teak.

The paddle steamers took us to another railhead and we journeyed on again by train through what must have been northern Assam. Eventually we detrained, and proceeded by lorry to a transit camp, probably at Dimapur. The next stage of our journey was a terrifying one in lorries driven by daredevil Indian drivers who drove like maniacs up steep tracks cut into the side of the mountains, round hairpin bends, so that we could look down and see broken crashed lorries lying at the bottom, as a reminder of what could happen to us. It was so scary that some chaps were sick, but we learned later that those tracks had been cut by hand for us to travel along, as the Jap' had blockaded the passes, and in fact they were a miracle of engineering, as before there were no tracks at all, and the drivers travelled fast because of the possibility of enemy mortar fire.

Enemy aircraft were scarce since a few Spitfires and Hurricanes had appeared on the scene patrolling the skies, so we weren't needed as anti-aircraft, and our role now was bunker busting. The Japs were experts at digging bunkers and they had been improving on them for two years, so it was no mean task to winkle them out. Shelling alone wasn't enough to dislodge them at times, and more drastic measures had to be used, like flame throwers.

Mostly though we were used as infantry, advancing and digging in through all types of terrain, from bamboo thickets, to elephant grass, sharp bladed grasses about 8 feet tall or more, not the best place to get lost in, especially as we sometimes were covered with large red biting ants and wary of snakes, and large spiders whose webs seemed always on a level with your face. Rivers were forded by canvas boats when available, if not by the best way that we could. We were taught to make a float by removing our trousers, do up the fly and tie each leg into a knot, now wade into the water and holding the waist band in both hands let the trousers hang down your back with your arms over your shoulders, then suddenly dash them over your head into the water the legs will fill with air and stick straight up, rest your chin on the crotch and kick your legs, you have a homemade float. Similarly, to make a stretcher, button up two tunics turn them inside out, push two poles up through the inside of the tunics through the sleeves, and you have a strong stretcher. Bamboo has many uses and by copying the natives we made good use of it too.

There were often times when we had to make do with just one pint of water to last all day during the dry season. Some chaps though didn't have the strength of will power to preserve their ration, and would have an empty water bottle before anybody else, and then try to scrounge a drop from their mates. We had somehow got cut off from the main body once when out on patrol, and we were out of water, and not likely to find any. The situation was serious, we were gasping and on the verge of heat stroke. While crossing a dried up river bed known as a nalla, we saw a wild water buffalo further along the nalla, snorting and digging with his front hooves at the sandy floor. We said to each other, "That blighter can smell water!" So we set to work digging with our entrenching tools, and sure enough there was some dampness and then mud, and then water, we made a pool and stood back to let the buffalo have his drink after all he may have saved our lives, when

71

the water had cleared we filled our water bottles, popped in a chloride tablet and carried on our way, we had learned how to find water when in need. Washing was a luxury, and the use of soap was forbidden as the smell could give our position away. Absolute silence was essential when in contact with the enemy, but using the wireless even with the volume turned right down and using earphones the high pitched pip pip of the Morse dots and dashes seemed louder than it probably was.

The Japs used to taunt us with maniacal laughter and screams often calling out girl's names, like Rosie or Mary, "Where are you Mary?" in the hope that we would get annoyed and reply thus revealing our position, so that he could use his mortars on us. The jungle is dimly lit in the daytime as the sunlight cannot penetrate the treetops very much but at night it is pitch black, and far more noisier than in the day, as then the predators are hunting for food. I was on guard one night under a big Banyan tree, these trees send down roots from their horizontal branches and they form another tree trunk, so making a form of arches like being in a cathedral, interesting in daylight but weird at night. I was on watch from 4am until 6am at which time I had to call the cook to light his fire and get the dixie on for "gun fire" as the early morning cup of tea was called.

It was pitch dark and I couldn't see a thing but I had a premonition that I was being watched, and that I wasn't alone. My ears told me that nothing unusual was moving about, as the cicadas were singing their shrill song, and if there had been, they would have stopped, they were my warning device. I stood with my back to the tree trunk guarding my rear, still with this eerie feeling that all was not well. It gets daylight about 6am and you may remember that Kipling said the dawn comes up like thunder over China across the way! Well it does, first you hear the jungle cock-birds crowing, they are the ancestors of our domestic farmyard fowl, they are joined by the wild peacocks screaming, and the next thing you know it is daylight.

I looked about me and all seemed well until I looked up into the dark branches of the tree and there above me were two green eyes, I backed away slowly and went over to the slit trench where Tommy Lee the cook was sleeping, and shook him awake saying, "Come on Tom time to get the dixies on, but fix your bayonet we may need it!" "Why, what's up?" said Tom in his Scouse accent, I said, "Come along and I'll show you." So together we went across to where I had been standing, right where Tom had his cook house, and I said "Look up there" hoping that it had gone away."

Ruddy Hell!" said Tom "I'm not lighting a fire under that, what shall we do?" We couldn't fire a shot, so I suggested that he should cover me with his bayonet, while I rap the tree with my rifle butt and hope that he takes off, so that is what we did and all that I could see up there in that dark tree was the impression of a black body streaking away, so I can only suppose that it was a black panther, a little too close for comfort, it was one of the longest guards that I have ever been on. That creepy feeling is a bit off putting I must say.

I had another encounter with wild animals once back in India. I had a type of skin disease that can only be cured in the cool mountain air, so I was transported to a hospital high up in the mountains, which turned out to be an old stone built barracks converted into a hospital for skin diseases. After checking in I was shown to this one room separate block, that was large enough to take 6 beds but there was only one bed made up, the others were stacked up in a corner so I was on my own. There was an empty fireplace, and I had noticed some fire wood as I came in it was cold so I went out to gather some, and a little terrier dog made friends with me, so I coaxed him in and put some sacking down by the fire for him. Now I had some company even if it was only a dog. There were no curtains and the door was a glass panelled French window that opened out to the outside but wouldn't close properly. I went off to sleep. Suddenly there was a commotion and howling outside and I woke up with a start to bright moonlight, the dog had dashed out of the door, and on looking out I saw some big dog like creatures prowling about. I thought "My Goodness they look like wolves" and I stacked the bedsteads up against the door and went back to sleep. In the morning the Indian orderly was knocking to be let in "Kiswaste Sahib?" he said meaning what for? Indicating the barricade, and I told him. "Oh acha thickhi"= alright. He said, "Wolves!" Apparently they came scavenging on a moonlit night round the dustbins.

Incidentally I was there for a few days, and met two of the lads that were on our mess deck, and who I hadn't seen for the many months that we had been in India. Someone hailed me as I was strolling through the grounds one day, and there was this chap with his face all bandaged up so that I couldn't recognize him. He said "I know you from H deck on the troop ship." "Good Heavens mate, what ever happened to you?" I said, and he began to cry and said I'm so miserable, they tell me that I shall never get better as long as I stay in this country, but they won't send me home. I tried to cheer him up telling him that it was only a matter of time, and that they would soon be sending him home, look at it this way you are comfortable here, just take it easy until that time comes.

England really did seem like another world in that alien place, and I felt so sorry for him. Another day a tall gaunt looking chap was walking towards me all skin and bones, and I thought I know that face, "Hello" said I calling him by name, "where the devil have you been all this time?" He too started crying. "Oh mate," he said, "I was daft enough to go to those brothels in Bombay, and I got a 'full house'. The trouble is that my marriage allowance has been reduced to pay for the treatment, and my wife has been informed of the reason why, I can never face her again, and I am seriously contemplating suicide, life has no meaning anymore, I am so ashamed." Well! What can you say to a chap in those circumstances? I am no counsellor, but I spoke earnestly to him at some length about the fact that while there is life there is hope, and his wife would forgive him eventually and so on, I don't suppose that it did any good but I tried to tell him the things that he would want to hear, that it was a long treatment true but it could be cured in time, so hang on in there. I saw them both every day until I was discharged back to my unit. I don't know how they got on, but I do know that some severe cases of V D never did go home. Men were stricken with all kinds of illnesses, some types I expect never heard of before, and some psychological, strange things happened a man might suddenly attack his best friend, and just as suddenly become normal again.

I knew that Gwen was working in a R.O.F. (Royal Ordinance factory) a dangerous job, but that is all that I knew, and one day I picked up a newspaper, which reported a R.O.F. explosion in the Midlands. The next morning, I found that the side of my face had swollen up. The young Captain that I was driving for as a Dv'r Op' said "Hello Kemp what have you been up to, fighting?" "I said "No I think that it must be an insect bite." The next morning, the swelling on that side had gone down and reappeared on the other side of my face, so I decided to go sick. On being admitted to the doctor, before I could say anything, he said, "Well what are you worried about?" I thought that was a strange question, so I replied, "nothing much except getting back home away from this rotten dump!" He wasn't satisfied with that, and said "Now come on something is worrying you, what is it?" So I told him about the paper that I had found. "Don't be daft" he said, "you know that no news is good news. You would have been notified by now if anything was wrong, so clear off and stop worrying!" I did that and my face soon returned to normal.

There was a chap from the Island in our unit, and I made his acquaintance quite by accident, we were watching the lads playing football one day, and this chap was standing near me shouting familiar Island football slogans, so I asked him where he came from. Oh you wouldn't know it he said, it's a little village on the Isle of Wight called Bembridge. I laughed and said of course I know it I am from Ryde! Lennard was his name, and he was also a Dvr' Op' so we had something in common from then on. When at long last Len had served his time and was due to return to the U K, I who had joined them as a reinforcement had to stay on a while longer. I well remember the night before he was due to depart, we sat talking of home, and I had a lump in my throat at the thought of him going all the way back. Just think Len I said, you are going all the way home to our dear old Island, and I am stuck here still in action, I could get killed yet. He said don't worry mate, I'll tell you what, as soon as I have seen my folks, I'll go and see yours, and tell them that I left you fit and well. He was as good as his word and for that I am eternally grateful!

Mountbatten

We had a visit from Lord Louis Mountbatten the supreme commander one day, we were back behind the lines, and we could tell that something unusual was afoot, there was a lot of fuss and bother as the officers had been warned that he was coming. We were all paraded and inspected and drawn up on parade when he arrived, but he wanted none of that, a soap box was produced which was carried for the purpose and he stood up on that and said alright Lads, break ranks and gather round me, sit on the ground and light up if you have any and if you haven't don't look at me! He then went on to say that there were going to be some changes made for the better, that he was aware that we were told nothing and didn't know what was going on, who was on our left or right, in front or behind us, or where we were going, but that situation was going to alter.

He was quite right, up until then we were never told anything, and rumours aren't good for morale. He said that we would receive a news-sheet once a month from SEAC (South East Asia Command), called "Dekko" (the Hindi word for Look) telling us what was happening. He also said that there will be no slackening off during the monsoon, but we will continue to fight right through it. Also from then on if we came up against stubborn resistance from the dug in enemy, and we couldn't dislodge them, we were to push on and abandon them, leaving them without supplies, to get on with it. We gave him three cheers when he departed. He had cheered us up a bit.

We had an old portable gramophone, but eventually only one record which was Bing Crosby's White Christmas, very appropriate in that heat and of course every time that I hear it now, which so far has been every Christmas since, it reminds me of that time when we had no needles and had to use a thorn instead, it worked but very quietly. We the Dvr' Ops' could tune in to music but only by disobeying the rules, as we were supposed to stay on frequency all the time, in case of emergency. There wasn't much to find by searching the ether anyway except Indian wailing and we didn't want that. Tokyo Rose was good for a laugh though.

We used to charge our twelve volt batteries with a little petrol driven generator and once I tripped over a lead that was lying along the ground causing the crocodile clip to pull off making a spark which exploded the gassing battery. This caused an enquiry and it looked as though I would have to pay for it, but I got away with it because it was an accident.

After a long and hard struggle, at last the Japs were on the retreat and we were chasing them. If we came up against any firm resistance from well dug in Japs, we simply by-passed them and left them to starve or surrender. Up until this time surrender wasn't a consideration with them as they would rather die for their emperor, who they worshipped like a God, they considered it a disgrace to surrender. That is partly why they treated their prisoners of war so badly. They depended a lot on food that they stole from the natives by force, as they could survive on a hand full of rice a day, but now the cupboard was bare, as the rice harvest hadn't been gathered yet. We were supplied by parachute drops from the air and the Dakota supply planes often had difficulty in finding us beneath the canopy of the trees, it wasn't always possible to find a clearing, so some times we had to clear one ourselves. We would lay out crosses using parachutes and prepare a beacon ready to light to show the wind direction, and then radio our position to base. They would give us an ETA (estimated time of arrival) and we would listen for the sound of their engines approaching then light the beacon so that the smoke might show our position and direction of wind.

The whole thing was fraught with danger in case the enemy was in the vicinity. The plane or planes would have to come in as slow and low as they dared, while the crew known as packers struggled and sweated to push the load out of the open rear end, or through the door. Bear in mind that those planes were unarmed and unescorted. Sometimes they were unable to find us and had to give up and try again another day. This operation was especially difficult in the monsoon season, because of the poor visibility and strong winds. Sometimes the enemy would try to get the supplies first and if it was much off target, they could get there before us and then a battle royal would ensue, to get the much needed supplies.

If we were too eager and rushed out to get them before they had landed, there was the danger of being hit by free falling goods that didn't need a parachute, like bales of hay for the mules, and things that wouldn't damage. They would thump down just missing us.

I remember once some chaps secreted a canister of rum behind the bushes intending to keep it for themselves and that night they had too much of it and couldn't keep quiet in their fox holes, until a little Geordie fellow jumped out into no-man's land shouting "Come on you yellow buck toothed slant eyed bow legged bastards come and get me!" His mates had to rush out and drag him back in and gag him. Of course there were enquires made in the morning, but they had buried the canister by then and claimed that Geordie had a touch of the sun and had succumbed to a moment of madness. This excuse wasn't entirely believed, but there was no evidence of stolen rum and they got away with it.

Those brave airmen took terrible risks, sometimes being fired on from the ground, and they were unarmed if there had been a Jap fighter about. We fully realized that without them we couldn't have survived like we did. Supplies by mule were all very well, but they were too slow and base too far away.

The trouble was that Burma was a very mountainous and hilly country and the hills always ran across our line of approach so that we were on a switchback constantly climbing up and down the other side, it was a great relief when we got near to Mandalay as we were coming down onto the planes and it was much easier going, but we had to fight our way in to Mandalay against stiff opposition. The Pagodas were many and beautiful, some with reclining Buddha's, but mostly the Buddha's were sitting upright, legs crossed under them, with plenty of wind charms, prayer wheels, big brass gongs, joss sticks and incense and all sorts of bells. Attended by monks in saffron robes with their heads shaved some as young as school boys.

The Japs would sometimes impersonate bullock cart drivers with their weapons under the load, in order to sneak through our lines, so if we were suspicious we would challenge the driver, who would prove that he was a Burman by pulling up his "Longi" or skirt that they wore, to show that their legs are tattooed from the knee upwards on their thighs all Burmese men have these tattoos, so that was a convenient way of proving that they were genuine.

Walking Wounded

I had the misfortune of badly damaging my teeth one day, I was down on one knee operating the wireless with earphones on. With my rifle across my knee to keep my hands free, when Jap opened up on us with mortar fire, and when you are in the process of scribbling down a message there is no way that you can duck. Anyway a heavy branch came crashing down across my shoulders, forcing my mouth on to the rifle and breaking off some teeth and it was very painful. I had to stick it though for several days before they could fly me back to an aid post.

That trip was quite an adventure. It was a little American single wing aircraft which carried one stretcher case and one walking wounded, me! The pilot was a big fat American sergeant smoking a cigar and the Jazz on his wireless made talking impossible, but it was interesting to look down and see things from that angle. When we landed I said "Thanks for the ride Joe, just like being in a taxi." he said "Yeah I was a foot slogger once before I got wise, but it's mighty hard on yer arse!"

I joined the long queue at this tented hospital and two white-coated orderlies came along assisting a heavily bandaged Gurkha between them and as he passed I gave him our usual greeting of "thickhi Johnny" to which he replied as usual "thickhi Sahib" and continued on his way. I thought no more about it until one of the orderlies came hurrying back and said "Here, do you know that Gurkha?" I said "No, one Gurkha is the same as another to me." He said "Well he knows you, and we can't pacify him until you come up and tell him how the battle is going." I said well I can't speak Gurkhali but I'll try, so I tried to tell him that all was well, he could speak a little English, Hindi, and Urdu so we got along but it wasn't long before they took him through for treatment. He must have been from our sector and recognized me.

The Gurkhas make fun of their wounded and call them "shushti wallas" (lazy men or lead swingers). I am told that they have no word for fear in their vocabulary, I don't know if this is true, but I wouldn't be surprised. I have been told that their initiation ceremony into manhood is to decapitate a bull with one stroke of the Kukri, a curved knife, their favourite national weapon. I would rather have a Gurkha as a friend than foe.

Darjeeling

Now at last we are due for leave again, and this time we are given a choice of places to go. Fred and I chose Darjeeling up in the Himalayas in Nepal. 7000 feet above sea level, 370 miles from Calcutta. As before, we were asked how much money we would like to take, and that question always caused a chuckle. I should point out that all the time that we were in action we received no pay in cash as we had no use for it, instead it was credited to us, so that we had built up quite an amount of savings. We were flown out in an old Dakota aircraft with no thought of comfort, there were no seats in fact we were sitting on the floor in our jungle green uniforms, and when we lifted up over the mountains we were shivering with the cold but we didn't care, we were going on leave, and determined to enjoy every minute of it. We landed at Comilla transit camp on the border of India, and spent the night there, here we were kitted out with khaki drill bush shirts, shorts and slacks, our pass, and travel warrants, and off to the train for Calcutta. Here we changed trains going north, right up to the foothills of the mountains, and then changed to the narrow gauge mountain railway, to ascend the mountain. This was a sturdy little train built in Glasgow, which pulled several coaches and we were told that this railway was one of the Seven Wonders of the World. Soon we were to find out why. The gradients were so steep that the train would take a run at it until the wheels started slipping and by the way there was a native sitting on the front of the engine scattering sand on the line, to help them grip. Then the points would be switched behind us, the brakes were released, and the train would rush backwards up another slope as far as it would go, and then down again to give it momentum, and give it that extra speed to take it over the top. It was every bit as thrilling as a Blackpool switchback! We went round in tight turns so much in fact that at one time the engine was actually over the last coach.

The scenery was fantastic the vegetation changing the higher we went with flowering shrubs like azaleas and rhododendrons in a blaze of colour, and in the background was the snow covered Kanchenjunga mountain range the sun glistening on the snow, and the wind blowing a wisp of snow like smoke all of the time, off of the top. The weather was lovely, to us it was like an English spring, even to the call of the cuckoo, and everywhere there were flowers of all kinds. We were quartered in a rest camp and there were no restrictions, we could come and go as we pleased.

Fred and I became friendly with two American GI's from Texas, and we hired ponies nearly every day to ride up around the foothills. The little rosy faced children were full of mischief and would creep up behind us to smack the pony to startle it and then laugh heartily at our reactions, that to them was great fun. There were lots of pine trees and the sturdy men were doing their logging the old fashioned way, to saw the logs into planks they had a saw pit with a crosscut saw one man would be above and one below and they would saw away like that for hours.

To view Mount Everest, it was necessary to set out just before daylight to a view point called Tiger Hill by pony in order to see the sun rising, and catch the changing colours on the snow. The hired ponies were trained pack animals and always walked on the very edge of the narrow mountain tracks, because of the wide loads that they were used to carrying, so that you were constantly worried in case they slipped and fell down the mountain taking you with them, but if you happened to be fortunate and there was no mist, the panorama was stupendous, and well worth the journey.

The people were Sherpa's and Gurkhas, although there appeared to be many Tibetans in their big fur hats and boots, and we saw an occasional Yak, the ox-like beast of burden with big wide horns, and shaggy long hairy coats. The men folk seemed to spend a lot of time at gambling games and would get quite excited about them. They were sturdy people though and it wasn't unusual to see a large bundle of wood with two bow legs under it progressing up a steep slope. They had a wide band of material round the load on their backs coming up round their forehead, it is no wonder that they made such good porters for the mountaineers. They were used to it, and you had to be, the air was very thin up there. There were prayer flags everywhere, even hanging on the trees, but this was indeed a beautiful place. The tea plantations made employment for many of the population, it was interesting to see the women picking the tea from the bushes and tossing it over their shoulder into a basket on their backs, again held on by a broad band round their foreheads. We were able to buy some tea through the firm, and they sent it to our home address, and I was surprised to find that my mother had kept the packaging, when I returned home.

Return to Unit

All too soon our leave was up and reluctantly we had to return, but we had enjoyed it very much, and if ever I had to return to the Far East again, I would choose Nepal as the place to go. When we got back to Comilla we were told that our unit had moved on and that we had to wait until we could get transport onwards so that it took us several days to catch up with them, they were still in the Mandalay area, but were soon moving on again. In fact, we criss-crossed the country south of that area. We pushed through all sorts of rough terrain and forded rivers. Most of us had dysentery, with pains in the stomach and diarrhoea. This can be very awkward in a slit trench because there is no way that you can leave it, to go behind a bush, that would be a Jap snipers dream, so you just had to stay put and grit your teeth and dig a hole in the trench.

Time passed and season followed season, monsoons came and went and what miserable times they were, we saw plenty of action and most of us caught malaria as I did and I've had it on and off ever since.
One day I received some sad news from Gwen, her soldier brother Leslie had been killed in action in Italy. I felt so sorry for her, what can you say? I wracked my brains to find some comforting words to put in my letter, but words don't help, you need to be together at a time like that, to help each other through the sorrow. Her mother had lost two husbands and now Leslie. I don't think that her mother ever got over it. I had never met him as our leaves didn't coincide but I know that he was a grand fellow and when on leave was the life and soul of the party. His tragic death was a terrific blow to all who knew him and a very sad loss. He was serving with the 1st Royals Infantry and killed on 25-8-1944 at Anzio in Italy.

V. E. Day

Now at last great news, the war in Europe is over! We were delighted to hear that news and to know that our loved ones were safe from the terrible bombing, but for us no such luck, the order of the day was soldier on, we still had a long way to go.

Mum and Dad wrote me that they were buying a house in Wootton, a village just outside of Ryde and of course I was curious as to what it was like, they tried to describe it to me in their letters and I had a vague idea what the houses were like in that area.

As it was nearing the time that my comrades were due to return home, leaving us reinforcements behind, the Captain said to me I have just the job for you Kemp, the R.M.Ps (Royal Military Police). I laughed and said "Thank you very much sir, but I just couldn't join them after all that I have said about them," and he also laughed and said "Alright I'll see what else I can find for you." I heard no more and when the unit left I was attached to another outfit that was pushing on down to Rangoon. They were a rag time crowd but I didn't care I knew that it wouldn't be long until I too was on my way home.

V. J. Day

We had no sooner got to Rangoon when we got the stupendous news that America had dropped the atom bomb on Hiroshima and one on Nagasaki on 15-8-1945 and the Japs were forced to surrender. We are unable to relax though, as the stubborn so and so's wouldn't believe it and there was no way of letting the scattered Jap troops know. They wouldn't surrender anyway and would fight to the death regardless and there was always the danger of some demented uninformed sniper.

We had got to Rangoon so I was able to see the city such as it was. The big attraction of course was the Shwedagon Pagoda covered in gold, built in 585 BC, a pilgrimage point for all Buddhists. Oddly enough Rangoon translated means "End of conflict."

I had travelled the whole length of Burma and much of its interior and I was longing to get away. When eventually we got back to India, we learned that we were being demobilised according to our age and length of service and I was labelled 28 group, I taught the Char Walla to shout "Roll on 28 Group!" He didn't know what it meant but he kept shouting and so did I!

Coming Home

A troop ship was loading with 26 group men and found that it had room for 27 and some 28 group men so we were on the train again for the long journey to Bombay. I was on my way! The good ship Dominion Monarch was about to sail and we were impatient to leave behind all the heat filth and flies, as we travelled at long last, to Bombay. When we got aboard one chap took off his boots and threw them back onto the quay shouting I wouldn't take your rotten dust with me! That just about summed up our opinion of India. There was no waving farewell we couldn't care less how they fared.

The Mediterranean Sea was open now of course and so our journey home was nowhere near so long as our journey out. I was sitting at the mess table one day, it was February and misty and there was some excitement as the chaps had spotted something off the port bow, "What is this?" they were saying, "Is it France or what?" I ran up the stairs to the deck and my heart missed a beat, there looming out of the mist was the Nab Tower. I was home! We were entering Spithead from the English Channel, the Island was only a mile or so away.

We laid off Cowes roads for three days. I could see people walking along the promenade on the Island and I was sorely tempted to swim ashore. Eventually we docked unceremoniously in Southampton, no hero's welcome, no bands playing, nothing! There were a few people anxiously scanning the faces lining the rail, who probably still clung to the hope that their long lost loved one might turn up one day. We were sent to a demobilization centre, where you go in at one end a soldier and emerge a civilian. With what money that is due to you, a suit, coat and hat in a cardboard box and you are free to go home. On leaving the demob' depot, I thought at last I am back in the real world, but was I?

The feeling was strange and I thought "steady mate!" this is going to take time to get used to. Six years of soldiering is a long time and almost 4 years abroad left me feeling a bit strange, almost as if I didn't belong. I got off of the bus where my parents and sister lived, and walked to their gate and there bless their hearts, was a large Union Jack hanging from a pole out of the bedroom window. I knew that there would be a lot of fuss, but I thought well here goes and walked up to the door. I had written to them and Gwen of course, telling them when I hoped to arrive home and they were expecting me. They were all over me and there was some excitement with everyone talking and asking questions at once and there was quite a lot of local and family news to catch up on.

I told them about coming alongside at Southampton and how sad it was to see those people on the dock gazing up at the faces on deck in the vain hope of finding that certain person! Some women I was told, met every troop ship in their expectation of finding him.

I found that I was still very wary and watchful, old habits die hard and the first time that I walked down the High street a pneumatic drill started up near me and instinctively I dived into a doorway, the rata-tat-tat was so similar to a machine gun. I felt so foolish and pulled myself together and from then on I had to make a conscientious effort to simmer down and sort myself out, it was all so weird at first.

I sent a telegram to Gwen telling her that I was home, but unknown to me, her family was in the throes of moving and she couldn't get away, so I had another week to wait, but after all what is a week after all that time? To me it seemed like ages I was so looking forward to being with her again. I went to Portsmouth to meet her. She had never seen me in civilian clothes. She stepped off the train looking all round expectantly, but as we came face to face I don't think that she was certain who I was, apart from wearing civvies, I had lost a lot of hair and weight owing to the heat and my face was yellow through taking mepocrine tablets. I said "Hello Darling don't you know me?" And we fell into each other's arms. Shyly we got to know each other again. I had brought her some clothes from India, but having no idea of her size, of course nothing fitted her. This was disappointing but of course I should have known better.

Since we lived 200 miles apart, naturally we wanted to get married as soon as possible, although there was no chance of finding somewhere to live, but my job was on the Island so we would have to live with my parents in the meantime. The date was set for the 27th July 1946, so we saw the vicar to call the bans, but he was reluctant to do so, because Gwen was a Methodist, and I was Church of England. Anyway he did, but we decided to tie the knot at Gwen's chapel at her home village of Wolstanton, Stoke on Trent.

The Wedding

Come the great day, Gwen looked beautiful in a lovely long white wedding dress and veil.

There were two bridesmaids, a pageboy and the best man was her brother Raymond and a better man I have never met, before or since. We had a grand reception at the Methodist Hall and a good time was had by all. I shall never forget when walking into the Hall there was a hymn scroll on the wall, and the first words of the hymn were "Courage brother do not stumble"

A taxi had been ordered to take us to Blackpool on Honeymoon and when it arrived there was a woman in the front passenger seat and she was chatting on about married bliss as we drove along. We found out later that she was the driver's fancy woman going along for the ride!

We enjoyed a fortnight at Blackpool on the south shore and the first day that we were on the beach there was a strong wind blowing and a man on a horse came galloping along blowing a whistle and shouting, "get off the beach, get off the beach! " I said to Gwen "what's up with him?" She said, "Come on we have got to move the tide is coming in fast" and so it was with the wind behind it I have never seen the tide rush in so quickly. It is different at Ryde because we aren't open to the ocean.

The boarding house was comfortable and friendly and the food was good. When it came time for us to leave, the same old taxi arrived, the fancy woman wasn't in it but all the boarding house turned out to cheer us off and to our embarrassment the taxi wouldn't start! So they had to push it and off we went, we just had to laugh it off, but it all added spice to the adventure, and gave us something to remember and talk about for the years to come.

Back to Work

Now the honeymoon is over and it is back to reality. My spell of holiday was gone, and I had to start work. If you remember I had done 4 years apprenticeship when I was called up for war service. When I went back to see the boss, he said "You have got to do another year of apprenticeship".
I said "I can't do that, I'm married" and he replied, "well you shouldn't have got married then should you?" If ever a man came close to a smack in the mouth he did, but I had to keep my temper. I needed the job and I had no option but to comply, there were no other jobs to be had. I was shocked at his off-hand attitude to a returned soldier but I learned not to expect any gratitude. Those who had wangled their way out of the service through the war just didn't want to know and were not interested in an ex-service man. could it have been due to a guilty conscience? I think so.

As soon as we could, we put our name on the council housing list together with many others and waited our turn. All the time trying to get other accommodation of any sort, but there was just nothing to be had. Several times we built up our hopes only to have them dashed by someone beating us to it, or it was a case of keep it in the family, but we kept on trying.

Now we have some good news, Gwen is pregnant! My sister Myra is also pregnant so we have some happy events to look forward to and we redouble our efforts to find somewhere to live, but it is hopeless. There came a vacancy for a tinsmith in our meter repair shop and on application I got the job which at least had a living wage, but only just. I didn't dislike the job though it took some getting used to being inside all the time.

Barry Is Born

Our son Barry was born on 23rd July 1947, during one of the hottest summers that we have ever experienced, a time for celebration except that we were still living with my parents
.

Living with in-laws is not an ideal situation for a young mother, no matter how tolerant each may be, there is bound to be a difference of opinion and petty irritations arise, which magnify as time goes by and we were desperate to get away. Our bonny bouncing baby was coddled, fussed over and thoroughly spoiled until he turned night into day. He would sleep peacefully all day and scream for attention all night. The Doctor told us that was the trouble he was thoroughly spoiled by all the grown-ups in the house we had to get away.

At last one of my workmates came to our rescue he knew an old lady who lived alone in a six roomed house with a basement. She used to do bed and breakfast but was now too old to do it anymore and he persuaded her to let us have the two top rooms with a box landing big enough to put a cooker in. The large front room became our living room with a view out to sea and the back room became our bed room, and the sink was in there. I was so relieved that I ran the gas supply up to a meter and cooker, and plumbed in the sink at my own expense. The toilet was on the ground floor and to get the coal for the fire it was necessary to go out of the front door, round the side of the house and down some steps into the little back yard and back.

The little old lady, let's call her Miss B' would stay down in the basement all day right up until midnight. We were quite near to the town hall clock, and every night as the clock struck 12 o'clock she would stump up the uncarpeted stairs to her bedroom on the ground floor. She suffered badly from asthma and would cough and wheeze loudly at the effort of climbing the stairs.

The baby's cot was in the bedroom with us and the first night when we put him to bed he started playing up as usual. I said to Gwen there is only one way to cure this nonsense, we will have to harden our hearts and ignore him, we couldn't do that before because my mum would interfere, but we had to do it, so we let him cry, he had a powerful pair of lungs and it was all that I could do to prevent Gwen from going to him. It was agonizing for both of us and caused some friction but it worked. He got the message that he wasn't going to win and he eventually went quiet, then I let Gwen go in and settle him down and we had no more trouble to settle him at night. The actual date that we moved in to the flat was October 1948, and Barry was 15 months old. We were very glad to get it despite the drawbacks and we happily settled down.

It was near the esplanade and Gwen was able to take Barry for walks by the sea and on to the sands. As I said, the landlady was an old spinster suffering from asthma and her breathing was getting worse. Every night regularly as the clock boomed the strokes of midnight, we would hear her stumping slowly up the stairs from the basement, the effort would cause her to stop at the top and take rasping gasps for breath and we got used to the sound. I have reason for describing this ritual, as one day when I came home from work, I heard her gasping for breath in her bed room and she sounded as though she was in distress, I told Gwen and she went down to see if she could do anything for her. It was obvious that she was very poorly and I went for the Doctor who had a practice not far away. He came and gave her an injection, but he had no sooner left the house when she ceased breathing altogether and appeared to have died. I rushed after the Doctor again and he came back and confirmed that she had died and wrote out the death certificate.

We notified her relatives and retired to our flat, shaken up at what had just taken place. We retired to bed as usual and dropped off to sleep, but we both shot up and hugged each other as the strokes of midnight were booming out and we once again heard the thump of her foot steps up the stairs and that horrible rasping, wheezing gasp of asthmatic breathing. At the twelfth stroke of the clock the breathing stopped never to be heard again, or was it? We couldn't believe our ears or understand what happened, we only know that it wasn't a dream, as we both experienced it and to us it was very real. The house was sold and the other rooms were let off. A young couple, Gerry and his wife, rented the ground floor and what was once the old ladies bedroom became their living room and kitchen. Gerry and his wife soon became friendly with us and one day unthinkingly I told them about the events on the night that Miss B' died and thought no more about it.

Gerry was working a lot of overtime until late in the evenings and his wife would spend her evenings with us until he came home. Gerry came home as the town hall clock was striking midnight one night and as he was approaching along the corridor to the kitchen, he heard the sound that I had described to him coming from the room. He pounded up the stairs to us and said "Here Hilt' I've heard that ghost!" he was panting and white in the face. I laughed and said "don't be daft, take more water with it!" "No he said I'm not kidding, I heard it as plain as it could be, I'm not going down there on my own, come with me please!" So off we went creeping down the stairs and there was the sound coming from the room. "What ever shall we do cried Gerry, I can't go in there." I pushed open the door and there on the stove was the kettle on a low light gurgling just off of the boil, making a noise just like the rasping wheeze and the mystery was solved.

Dumpy and Kay

Gerry and Dorothy had a beautiful little three-year-old daughter named Pauline, but her mother didn't seem to have much idea how to look after her and Gwen tried to help her.

One day Dorothy said to Gwen "I'm bored with nothing to do, if I got a full time job, would you like to look after (Dumpy)?" as they called her. "If I pay you?" Gwen was only too pleased and would have done it for nothing. So Dorothy got a job in the amusement arcade on the sea front and insisted on giving Gwen half of her wages. She didn't want the job for the money, she was just bored with being at home.

So we looked after Dumpy and enjoyed having her she was such a dear little thing. Shortly after that, a woman came to the door who we didn't know and she had with her, her little auburn haired 3-year-old daughter. She said "Are you Mrs. Kemp? I hear that you like children!" Gwen of course replied "Yes who doesn't?" To which she replied, "Would you like to look after mine?" Kay was her name and of course Gwen couldn't refuse, so we had a readymade family. Kay was so good that you could almost forget that she was there and Gwen loved having them.

Another young couple moved in to the floor below us. Sid and Joy and they were very friendly and they had a television set. Black and White of course as they were in those days, in their infancy then and there were not many about. There was only one channel, from Alexandra Palace, we were invited to view it from time to time and it was one of the wonders of the age.

Joy used to hang her washing across the landing and if they had a tiff, her underwear would be at one end and his at the other. We could always tell when they had made it up, because his and hers would be hung together again! They also had a bathroom and Sid wanted to hang a mirror on the wall, so he borrowed my electric drill and got cracking, the next thing that we knew he was shouting Hilt' where do you turn the water off? He had drilled into a water pipe, so I soldered it up for him and re-plastered the wall, no harm done.

He was able to get some veneers from a friend of his and was making some fine marquetry pictures with them, which I admired, so he said, "Why don't you have a go?" I said "Oh I don't think that I could do that" and he said "go on you'll be surprised; I'll show you how." So I had a go making my own cutting tools and made some pictures, being quite pleased with the result and I found that it was a nice quiet hobby for a flat dweller.
Dorothy and Gerry eventually moved away and the landlord's brother moved in, they were friendly but we didn't have much to do with them.
We had a good view out of the window down the street and on out to sea so that we could watch the big liners come by going into Southampton and a marvellous sight they were. Also at the review of the fleet all the naval vessels would be lit up and dressed all over at night. The yachts too with their coloured spinnakers, made a pretty picture. There was always something to see out there.

In the 1950s were the days of cheap excursion tickets by rail from London's Waterloo station to Portsmouth and thence across the six miles of sea to the Isle of Wight. At that time some of the older ferries were still paddle steamers superseded by more modern screw driven steamers. They used to arrive heavily laden at frequent intervals alongside Ryde pier and the crowds of Londoners would stream down the gang planks inappropriately dressed for the seaside, most of the men in their pin stripped (Demob suits) some with knotted handkerchiefs on their heads as protection from the sun. They of course brought some prosperity to the island for the shopkeepers and landladies of boarding houses who incidentally all seemed to hail from Bolton, Manchester, or London. Often there were so many holiday makers that ordinary householders could do bed and breakfast as a side line. As a consequence of all this influx the beaches would be crowded and the ice cream kiosks would do a roaring trade. The coaches too would run trips to the island beauty spots. On their return to the ferries, they would be queuing as thick as flies all down the pier waiting to get on a boat.

Nationalisation

Now that a Labour government had come to power, the Gas industry was nationalized and this gave us a rise in wages straight away. A central office was set up in Ryde and we suddenly found that we had strangers walking about in smart suits, apparently doing nothing, and we thought "Oh yes, jobs for the boys are being created."

We found ourselves being bossed about by an ex- naval officious type, who obviously didn't know gas from fresh air, or what to do with it and proved it every time that he opened his stupid mouth. He got his ideas from picking the brains of skilled men and claiming them as his own, but he had the power to sack good men and did so if they opposed him. He was a blustering bully and I had met his type in the service before and knew that the only way to deal with him was to stand up to him and not to back down. He didn't like anyone whistling and knowing this, I walked into the office one-day whistling. He immediately said, "Stop that row Hilton" I replied "Don't be so damned miserable" and he laughed and fortunately he didn't meddle with me at all after that and I was able to keep out of his way.

One day I was called into the office and asked if I would be prepared to relieve a meter cash collector who was getting married and going on honeymoon for a fortnight. The snag being that it was at Ventnor which is a small town situated south of the Island, built on the face of a very steep hill overlooking the sea and meant travelling by train, every day and being away all day. I was puzzled as to why they had picked me as I hadn't done that kind of work before and said so.

"Oh don't worry about that," they said, you will be shown what to do. So I accepted the job thinking that it may lead to better things and I was keen to get on. Before nationalization there was no chance of promotion at all. Any way this was only a temporary thing but it may be my chance to show them what I could do. So I showed up at Ventnor showrooms and reported to the manager there a happy go lucky jovial little chap who I took a liking to straight away, his name was Toby and he soon put me at ease. He showed me how to empty a meter and work out the rebate, how to book the cash and bank it. He was a wizard with figures and could add up three columns of figures and put the answer at the bottom in a flash.

"Don't worry, if you are in any doubt, just come to me" he said "and I will put you straight." So I got on with the job to the best of my ability and found that I could do it alright. The biggest snag was getting used to the hills. Ventnor is built on extremely steep hills and it was hard work walking around. Sometimes the road would be up on a level with the roof tops and you had to go down steep steps and back up again and do the same again next door and so on all along the road. The fronts of these houses were facing out to sea with lovely views. I felt sorry for the Postman but you get used to it. I went down one flight of steps to the back door and there was no reply but there was a big St Bernard dog there and I made a fuss of him while I was knocking on the door. There was no one at home so I turned to go back up the steps but the dog had other ideas, he guarded the steps and growled every time I came near, I kept talking to him wondering how I was going to get out, when I noticed a shed in the corner of the yard, so I opened the shed door saying come on then boy and he ran in.

What a relief, I closed the shed door and departed. I also had to cover the country districts and villages, so I had to use my bike'.

My efforts must have been appreciated because shortly after his return from honeymoon, this chap was promoted to salesman and I was offered the job full time and though I didn't much care to be away all day, I accepted, as I got on well with Toby and I owed a lot of my success in the job to him. As time went by, we saw many changes owing to nationalization. The most worrying one being redundancy, every town had its own gas works and administration staff in the private days, but now we were going to be centralized and although they had created a large office in Ryde, there would have to be a sort out, to cut down on the white collar workers known as Staff and I was now Staff! Each gas works had their own Collectors and Meter Readers, so that there were far too many, as now just a few were going to cover the whole Island, which meant redundancy for quite a lot and we were very much in suspense as to who would get the chop! I was the last one to become a Collector, so logically, I should be the first to go. I managed to survive the first sort out as it mainly concerned men approaching retiring age. We were now travelling round together in a large van working the Island town by town. Now came another sort out and I survived again. The Island was now administered from a central office in Portsmouth. I was sent over there to a lecture once and there was a map of the area on display. I said to the instructor "There is something missing here isn't there?" "Why, what do you mean?" he said. I replied "I happen to come from the Isle of Wight and there is no sign of it here." "Oh" he said "that is a suburb of Portsmouth!" This annoyed me and I said "Oh is it well just you try walking to it!" Time passed and we were lulled into a false sense of security, for once more we were called into the office for a sort out and the worries started again. We were all chaffing each other as we nervously waited to be called individually. The interviews were taking place upstairs in the Board Room, the Holy of Holies. The chaps called before me, were coming back, some smiling, others looking glum, to tell us how they got on, they said that it was like a court martial up there and I was reminded of the old army saying "at least they can't make me pregnant". When it came my turn, I marched up the stairs as though I couldn't care less, but fully prepared to get the boot! You entered at one end of this long room and at the other end was a long table with the inquisitors sitting along it facing the victim, who had to walk right across the room to stand at the centre of the table facing them, I was reminded right away of that picture called "When did you last see your father!"

Promotion

Anyway they greeted me with smiles and the spokesman started making a speech praising my efforts and saying that I had earned promotion and would become a 'Specials' man. Later called Inspector. This meant that I would have to cover the Island sorting out any problems concerning meters and would get a substantial rise as from now. Well I was stunned and could hardly take it in. I thanked them very much and they said "No, we thank you, you have earned it," and I thought what did I do to earn it? I was in a daze and about turned and marched towards the door, but it was the wrong door! I opened it and walked in to the broom cupboard and closed the door behind me! I stood there in the dark and thought "I can't stay here" and came out again. I said "Sorry gentlemen, I am not familiar with the layout of this place". The looks on their faces said "My God, what have we done to choose him?" I came back to the waiting room and told them about my blunder and that helped to break the ice for them and they had a good laugh! The duties of a "Specials Man" later called Inspector, were many and varied, I would have to cover the whole Island on my own, and a vehicle would be provided.

Although I had an army license, this wasn't valid, so I took six lessons with the school of motoring, courtesy of the gas board, took the test and passed first time. Now I was eagerly awaiting the arrival of a vehicle, but when it came I had a shock, instead of a van, it was a powerful motorbike with a side box in place of a side car. It already had L plates on and the man who delivered it showed me the controls and departed leaving me to get on with it, which of course I had to do. I didn't have a license for a motorbike, so I had to apply for another test, which I also passed first time.

I had to phone the office morning and afternoon for emergency jobs like jammed coins, or full boxes etc. on any part of the island. This was on top of my appointments for the day. I got along on the three wheeled motor bike quite well, though it was a bit tricky cornering, until you got used to it, but one fine day, I had my first mishap. Breezing along minding my own business, when overtaking a parked lorry on my near side, I was startled to hear a clatter behind me and I realized that I must have hit something, although I had felt no impact and looking back while pulling up, I saw a policeman sprawled in the road with his push bike on top of him. Well you can imagine, this was most disconcerting, especially as when I walked back there were three more policemen helping him up. I stood there apologizing and wondering where they came from, while they dusted their colleague down apparently none the worse for wear, but I don't know about his bike. While I was thinking that I would get shot with a rusty razor, one of the policemen took me by the arm with a grim expression on his face, saying "well young man, you had better come along with us to the station!" Then the mystery of where they had sprung from was revealed, we were outside of the back entrance of the police station. The three were coming on duty and my victim was going off duty. We marched up to a small office to fill in the necessary forms, while I got the third degree. This done they were suddenly all smiles, laughing and joking and offered me a cup of tea, which I gladly accepted, although I was still wondering what action would be taken. Quite suddenly after I had drunk my tea, one of them said "Well go on then lad, don't hang about, you can go." I said "Well what's the score then, aren't you going to charge me?" At this they laughed and said "No it was his own silly fault, we saw the whole thing, and he should have looked before riding out behind that lorry." What a relief, and although they had teased me a bit, I had to laugh!

The Dog

There was a tumble down little house, situated at the end of a long garden and the occupants, man, wife and three children used to roam the streets with an old pram calling out for scrap metal, rags and bones. Consequently, the garden was littered with junk and scrap metal among which roamed poultry and a very fierce lurched dog. To get to the house you had to walk up the length of the garden, avoiding any obstacles as you went, but only after the dog had been safely tied up behind the house. It was necessary to stand at the gate while the dog barked and made frenzied charges at the gate, until the occupants took notice and removed the dog for you to enter. On one occasion they had removed the dog and I set off up the path only to receive a blow at the back of my neck with an angry fluttering of feathers the cock bird had attacked me and I thought hello, they are ganging up on me!

The interior of the house was indescribably muddled and dirty, so that it was always a relief to get out again. The dog of course was a nuisance as often his barking was ignored, so that we just had to stand there until someone decided to let us in. I got my own back by accident late one winter's afternoon. I was counting the cash on the kitchen table by the light of a guttering candle in the draft of a missing window pane, when the lady of the house offered me a large steaming grimy mug of scolding hot tea. She placed this at my elbow and departed. There was no way I could drink out of that mug, so as soon as her back was turned, I threw the tea through the missing window pane all over the dog that happened to be there at the time. He yelped and "pen and inked" a bit and she said "What is wrong with that dog?" I said "Oh he must have trodden on something sharp I expect."

In order to quickly change the subject, I said "excuse me, but I seem to know your face, have we met somewhere before?" "Funnily enough" she said, "I was thinking the same thing, were you in the 392 Rees?" "Yes I was." I said. "Yes that's right, you were Provo corporal for a while at Northwood HQ" she said. "How did you know that I asked?" She laughed and said "Well I was the sergeant cook in charge of the cook house." I was astounded and wondered what had happened to all her training in hygiene and sanitation? I could only assume that she had lost heart in her present circumstances and given up trying. Anyway from then on we had something in common and were able to reminisce about old times, so that I think that she used to look forward to my visits.

94

The Scientist

The Chief Clerk called me into his office one day and said "Hilton, I would like you to make a special effort to read the meter at this address, as it is long overdue and no one has been able to gain entry." The address turned out to be a small bungalow on the outskirts of a country village. Arriving there that morning, I noticed how dilapidated and unkempt it looked from the road, the front garden overgrown with brambles and weeds, a wicket gate hanging on one hinge and a narrow path leading through the undergrowth to the house. I wondered what sort of person lived in this place and wandered up the path. There was no bell or knocker, so I rapped loudly on the door and as expected got no reply.

The correct procedure now was to leave a printed card stating our business and requesting that I might be admitted when I called again at a specified time, in this case at 2pm that day. I had many more calls to make as my area was far and wide, but I stopped off at the local store and enquired about finding someone in, were they out at work etc.? They laughed and said "You won't get in there, no one can, she is daft and won't let anyone in."
I arrived back there at precisely 2pm. Knocking on the door, I heard a slight noise and on peering through the window, I could just make out a little old lady standing in the corner. I tapped lightly on the window to let her know that I had seen her and beckoned towards the door.

Very hesitantly she came to her side of the door and in a timed voice said "What do you want?" I called back that I was the gas man who had left the card requesting to read her meter. "Oh my son," she said "I can't possibly let you in here, you don't realize the danger!" I thought 'softly, softly, catchy monkey.' "Why madam" said I, "what is bothering you?" "The Russians," she said, "They are over the road firing at me, you see those broken panes of glass, that is caused by sniper's bullets!" The window was made up of small panes of glass about six inches square, set in a metal frame from which the paint had peeled causing it to rust and swell thus cracking the glass. I knew that to argue on that point would only antagonize her and I must avoid that at all cost if I was going to gain her confidence. Obviously I would have to play along with her. I said "Look madam, I have been listening and I haven't heard a shot for some time, have you? I have been through the war and I have dodged sniper's bullets before, I am willing to take a chance if you are." "Would you really take that risk for me?" she said. "Yes" I said. "I'll tell you what, when you are ready, you open the door quickly and I'll dash in. Right when you are ready." She said, "Are you ready?" I shouted "Yes, now!" and she drew back the bolts and opened the door. I was in. She slammed the door and shot home the bolts.

Now the meter was at the far end of the bungalow, so holding her finger to her lips in a conspirator manner, she said "Follow me and keep down," I knew that I would have to continue playing her along if I was going to pull this off, so together we crouched down low to creep along under the windows, her glancing over her shoulder to see if I was following. Eventually we reached the meter and I recorded the reading, now I had to listen to her story. She said, "You see during the war I was a very famous scientist, and I wrote a white paper on aeronautics and Lord Brabazon came from Bembridge dressed as a bus conductor to take it to East Cowes, but on the way he was intercepted by the Russians and the outcome of that was the sputnik. Mind you" she said,"I don't take all the credit they did improve on it!" I tried to put her mind at rest regarding her fears, saying that the army would soon clear the Russians off and that she had no reason to worry, but I had already wasted too much time over that job and had to push on. I sauntered into the office the next morning and chatted about this and that and as if it had just occurred to me, I casually said to the Chief Clerk, "Oh by the way here's that reading that you asked me to get." "How the blue blazes did you get in there?" he exploded, "nobody has been able to, not even the health people". I said "ah it takes one to know one" and then I started to tell him the story and I noticed that the whole office had gone silent as they all listened in.

Apparently they all knew what the position was out there, but hadn't bothered to tell me, but I had the last laugh after all. The next morning the Chief Clerk again sent for me and said "It is like this Hilton, as you are the only one to get into that house, I want you to report your findings to the Medical Officer of Health at the Newport Town Hall." I said "Oh I don't like that I don't want to be the one to put her away!" If those people knew their stuff, they could have used the same tactics and got in there too, I think that I'll take a course in psychiatry, its money for old rope. "However, orders are orders, and I went to the Town Hall and repeated my story over again. I emphasized that the place was clean and tidy, but obviously the poor old lady needed care and reassurance. Shortly after that on passing the house I noticed a 'for sale' sign up, so they must have taken her into care. I wonder how they managed to get in to do that. This story just illustrates some of the situations that I used to get into.

One dear old soul had her bed in the front room down stairs, right in front of the meter cupboard and I used to have to pull it out with her in it to get at the meter. I used to say "Hello Gran how is you today?" and every time she would reply "Oh son they have just pulled me through again!" I reckon that she had been pulled through more times than a rifle barrel.

One house that I called at and while knocking at the back door I heard a moan and I looked through the window, I could see fleas jumping about in the rays of the afternoon sun, despite that I couldn't ignore that moan and I went in shouting gas man. There was an old sofa against the wall with what looked like a heap of old rags on it and the moan was coming from there, so going across I saw an old lady lying there and her face was blue. I said. "Are you alright my dear?" and she said "No, but don't tell Cuckoo, she will tell me off." I could see that she was very ill so I nipped along to the police station which was close by and told them about it, and I said "By the way, what did she mean by Cuckoo?" They laughed and said that was the nickname of the householder who lived mainly in cuckoo land. They called an ambulance and the old lady was taken care of.

I could always tell if a place was lousy, they would start biting at the top of my socks. I then had to undress in the empty bath and get deloused; it was just a hazard of the job!

We were delighted when Gwen told me the good news that she was expecting again, as we longed for a little brother or sister for Barry. After a few months though, things started to go wrong and Gwen wasn't well. One day her friend Eva came to spend the day with her and I had packed some sandwiches intending to stay out at work all day, but at about 10 O'clock in the morning, I was calling on a house boat on Bembridge embankment, a matter of about 4 miles from home. I got off of the motorbike and walked up the gangplank to the cabin door and raised my hand to knock it, but I stopped unable to do so. Suddenly I had an irresistible urge to go home and I just couldn't knock that door, I had to go home.

I about turned and got back on the bike with this thought hammering in my head, I must go home! I hurried as fast as I could and as I turned the corner of our street, there was an ambulance at our door. Gwen had willed me to come and had to plead with the ambulance driver to wait, saying I know that he will come, so I was able to see her briefly before they took her to hospital, she was having a miscarriage.

So close were we that we often knew what each other was thinking. That evening I was sitting by the fire, when I again got the call, it is the strangest feeling that I find hard to explain, I suppose that one has to experience it to understand. I collected a night dress and a few other things that I thought that she might need and set off. It was long after visiting time and even lights out at the hospital so what excuse could I have for going there? Also it was about 8 miles to the hospital, but that didn't stop me going.

Gwen had been offered a sleeping pill which she had refused, there is only one thing that will send me off to sleep she said, if only my husband could come and hold my hand! Arriving at the hospital I spoke to the night nurse on duty and made the excuse that I had brought a night dress in case she didn't have one. She was very understanding and asked me to wait while she took them along to the ward. When she came back she was smiling and said apparently she is expecting you, go on in, but only for a little while, we hugged each other and she said I knew that you would come, I willed it, so I sat by her bed holding her hand until she dropped off to sleep and I was able to creep away, sad to say it was a miscarriage and we lost the baby. The same thing was to happen on two other occasions and we were unable to have any more children, much to our sorrow, for Gwen loved children. We still had little Kay to care for though, as well as Barry of course. That sixth sense if that is what it was, cannot be denied and we instinctively were in harmony in our thoughts. I suppose that is the basis of a happy marriage. I only know that we were blessed in that sort of way and really feel sorry for those that are not.

Pets

Some people shouldn't be allowed to keep pets, as they either have no idea how to look after them, or they are too incompetent to care for them properly. I have seen them kept in appalling conditions. There were some houses that the Collectors and Readers refused to enter because of the conditions caused by pet's owners and so I would have to go instead.

In one house the meter was against the wall under the kitchen table, and an Alsatian dog had a litter of pups under there too. It was necessary to crawl in there to get at the meter. Naturally she was very protective of her puppies, but the silly woman said "Oh she is very placid, she lets me handle them, she won't mind if I am here." I said "Maybe she doesn't mind you because she knows you, but I am a stranger, and she couldn't be blamed for attacking me in defence of her pups, so you will have to coax her and her pups out before I go in" and although she was reluctant to do so, I insisted, and in the end that is what she had to do.

Most people are fond of cats, that is all well and good in moderation, but some irresponsible people allow them to breed unchecked so that eventually the house is full of them and they have to keep them in for fear of losing them, or because of complaining neighbours, consequently they aren't house trained and the result is appalling. It seems that the owners get used to the smell and are prepared to live with it. This is cruel to the cats that are clean and independent when properly looked after. These people dote on them and say aren't they lovely and expect you to agree. The RSPCA are usually aware of the circumstances, and keep an eye on them, but they cannot do anything unless they get a complaint from the neighbours.

At one house aptly named the wilderness, I was confronted with a goat asleep on the settee in the front room, while pigeons strutted about on the floor. There were also cats and dogs obviously not house trained, about the place, so you can imagine the state of the floor. Although I didn't comment, the lady of the house protested loudly that she wouldn't part with her animals for anyone! Of course I knew that our chaps had complained to her about the state of the place and she was on her guard expecting me to do the same, so I registered my disgust by keeping silent, as I knew that it would be a waste of breath anyway. I simply did my job and got out as quickly as I could.

I am no shrinking violet, but I cannot understand how people can voluntarily live in such a state of their own making, apart from the smell and filth, there are fleas and flies which spread disease. I used to put on a brave face and get on with it, the job had to be done but when you are emptying the meter and counting the cash and doing the booking in those conditions, there is no chance of holding your breath all the time and nowhere clean to put anything down. I often removed the cash box and took it all outside to work on the window sill in cramped conditions rather than stay in the house to do the job if the weather was suitable and get away as soon as I could!

I have special memories of one particular village in which I have worked, because of several unusual experiences that I had there. Calling at a certain house one day, the lady was in the front garden and let me into the front room where the meter was and while I was emptying it and talking to her there came a crash from the kitchen accompanied by loud swearing. The lady explained that it was only George who was fitting a water heater. I had only just started working in this area and had heard of George although I had never met him. He was the resident gas fitter, who having been born and raised in the village knew everyone. The villagers in turn knew him and were well used to his eccentric and unorthodox ways. He was a humorous sort of chap who was fond of a joke and chatting up the woman. This was my introduction to George who became a good ally, being so knowledgeable about the village and its inhabitants.

Further along the road I called at a big house where the people were obviously well off and was let in by a smart young lady. In the course of conversation, I mentioned George. "Yes" she said, "He is rather peculiar isn't he?" In her educated accent. "How so?" I said "Well" she said "Every time I meet him he seems to be up a lamp post and calls out "How would you like to come ferreting with me my dear?"

I knocked on a door one morning and to my amazement it was opened by a young lady wearing nothing but panties and bra. Oh I'm sorry she said, I thought that you were the insurance man!" where upon she went off and put on a dressing gown, apparently she didn't consider it necessary to do so for the insurance man!

There was one particular cottage where the Readers hadn't been able to get in for some time. When I called there I found a note pinned on the door, which read "Don't knock am in bed with Barry" I thought fancy, that's nice! Then I heard a noise in the kitchen and peered through the net curtains. There standing in a zinc bath absolutely naked was the lady of the house, she saw me at the same time and absolutely unabashed shouted that if I would wait a moment she would come to the door. She dried herself off and put on a dressing gown before letting me in. I apologized for disturbing her and emphasized the fact that her meter had been missed for a long time as she always seemed to be out when we called. She explained that she was a nurse on shift work and was either on duty or asleep when we called. When I queried the note, she laughed and said that the note was for her daughter and that Barry was her little grandson.
On one sad occasion a lady came running out of a house and called "Please help me my husband is very ill, and I don't know what to do!" I followed her up the stairs and her husband was lying in bed obviously quite dead. I went through the motions of testing for breath with a hand mirror and said that I thought that it was too late and asked her if she was on the telephone she said that she wasn't but her neighbour was. So I asked her to

put the kettle on, while I went next door and explained the situation to her neighbour. I telephoned the doctor while the neighbour went to comfort the poor lady and I went on my way.

The Cobbler

While chatting to George one day, I mentioned that I had a troublesome wart on my thumb. He suggested that I should visit old Jim the village cobbler, adding that Jim could charm warts. I thought that George was pulling my leg and told him so. I had heard that some people could charm warts, but thought that it was an old wives' tale and didn't believe it. George did believe it and pointed out that I had nothing to lose but the wart and I didn't want that anyway. The next time that I was passing the cobblers shop I summoned up the courage to go in feeling rather foolish.

Old Jim certainly looked the part. A little hunchback, he sat at his Last working on a shoe, a wizened little man wearing steel rimmed glasses and a leather apron and bib. Nervously I said "Good morning, what a lovely day." He peered at me over the top of his glasses and said "Well what can I do for you, young man?" "Well I stammered George tells me that you can charm warts." "Why have you got one?" he asked, I began to advance my hand to show him, but he quickly stopped me saying "No don't show me, I don't want to see it, you go away and forget all about it and it will be gone in a few days". I'll admit that this was a bit of an anti-climax, I didn't know what I expected but I thought that at least there would have been some sort of mumbo jumbo. I thanked him for his time and went back to work.
Now I had had this wart for some time and had always been conscious of it being there, however strangely enough I did forget all about it until a few days later when I realized that it was gone, there wasn't even a mark where it had been. Had our friend the cobbler had anything to do with its disappearance? The fact remains that the wart was there and a few days after my visit it was gone. The next time that I was in the village I called into his shop again, greeted him and asked if he remembered that I had visited him a few days ago about my wart? I then told him that it had gone and asked him how much I owed him? He smiled and said that it had cost him nothing and so I owed him nothing.

While chatting to him I looked around his little shop. Cobblers were so familiar in those days but sadly are few and far between now. The first thing that one notices about it is the smell of leather and polish that permeated the place. There were shelves with boots and shoes awaiting collection or repair, hanging around the walls were pieces of harness and saddlery. His bench was laid out with the tools of his trade and littered with scraps of leather, in one corner was an old fashioned sewing machine and in the other corner was a cage with an African parrot.

The Key

Once when out walking in our town, I indicated a woman on the other side of the road and told Gwen jokingly that I was sweet on her at school and that she was now married and had a nice little bungalow, her name was Dorothy and her husband was a musician in a dance band.

We had been on the council housing list for nearly four years and it was nearing our turn for a key to a council house. Gwen called at the town hall one day to check our progress and was surprised to see this Dorothy in the queue ahead of her and wondered what her business was. A new council housing estate was being built and we knew that it wouldn't be long before we would receive a key, as we were top of the list and had been notified that we would receive one on a certain date. We looked forward eagerly to the day when at last we would have our own little house. When that day came Gwen turned up at the town hall full of anticipation, but this Dorothy was again ahead of her and was given a key. When Gwen arrived at the desk, the clerk apologized and said that our key had been given to this Dorothy as they were in dire straits and we would have to be patient a little longer. Gwen said "I don't understand this, I happen to know that she has a nice bungalow." "Well I am told that she and her husband are sleeping rough" said the clerk, "but you had better take it up with the council, I can't help." It turned out that she had left her husband and was going with a German ex-prisoner of war and they were pleading that they were homeless and having to sleep in the recreation ground. The councillors had swallowed this bilge and allotted our key to them. Gwen was furious and canvassed the councillors telling them that the couple were not married, but they didn't want to know, she only found one councillor who was sympathetic, so nothing was done about it.

Our turn, for a key, came eventually of course, but I used to see this German strutting about with two Alsatian dogs as though he owned the place, He obviously didn't work and was living on the social security. We got on with our lives, but weren't very happy in that environment and resolved to find a place to buy as soon as possible. That house was a two up and two down, with a kitchen and toilet, with a small garden.

There was a door at the back which opened into under the stairs and was used as a tool shed. One day I made a Guy Fawkes for Barry and dressed it in an old suit of clothes and sat it on a chair in the tool shed. The baker came and finding no one in went to leave the loaf in the tool shed and received a shock to find this dummy sat up in the chair facing him. He said later that it nearly gave him a heart attack.

We had rotten neighbours each side of us and couldn't get away fast enough. So we had to save hard to afford a mortgage, to buy our own house at a future date.

The date that we moved into the council house was 16-10-1957. Life was the normal daily round, Barry had started school in 1952, and was growing fast. Our friend Eva, and her husband Len lived in the same street and they had two little girls who used to play with Barry.

Our happiest memories are when we were privileged to care for our three little nieces. Gwen's brother Harry's wife, had been taken seriously ill and had to go to hospital in the summer of 1958. As Harry was a full time male nurse, he was unable to look after his children. Vera had three married sisters, but Gwen jumped at the chance to care for them and Harry brought them to us from their home in Staffordshire.

They were Moyra, aged 13, Marilyn, aged 9 and little Yvonne aged 7. It must have been a big upheaval for them coming to a strange place so far from home and naturally at first they were home sick. Gwen and I did our best to make them welcome and settle them down. Telling them that this was their home for a little while until Mummy was better. Yvonne and Marilyn were able to attend the same school, but Moyra being older, had to attend another school.

We used to take them for walks in the woods gathering wild flowers and down to the beach to play on the sands. Eva's two girls Daphne and Valerie used to come and play with them and we still had Kay, so what with Barry and his mates, we had a house full at times. I remember once when I was off work on the sick, my boss came to the door and I asked him to wait while I cleared the front room of kids and they all streamed out past him as he stood on the doorstep. His eyebrows shot up and he said "My Goodness I didn't realize that you had so many children." I laughed and said "don't worry, they are only borrowed."

Although they got on fine and Gwen was in her element, I only wish that we had been better off so that we could have given them more treats. I had no car at the time and I remember that once we took them to Ventnor by train as a treat, the journey was fun, but when we got there, it was covered in thick sea fog and we couldn't see a thing, so we came home again, they enjoyed the train journey though.

We enjoyed having them as they were very good and never caused any bother, being sisters they were able to help each other, playing together and sharing each other's troubles. Happy times if it hadn't been for the anxiety over their mother's health. When the time came for them to go home we were sorry to see them go, but so pleased that Vera had improved so much that she was able to have them back.

We had a little dog at the time called Mandy and they made a terrific fuss of her and every time that the Ice cream man called, Mandy had to have one as well. The trouble is that she was petted and fussed over so much, that when they were gone, she missed them and would look for them so earnestly, that she would go up too little girls and finding that they were strangers she would snap at them and frighten them, so that we had complaints from their parents and she would do this even when on a lead, as we never let her roam loose, so in the end most reluctantly we had to have her put down.

Z.Call-Up

In the fifties, the international situation was such that a quarrel was going on over ownership of the Suez Canal. The Suez crisis was brought about when President Nasser of Egypt nationalized it and in an attempt to reassert international control of the canal, the British, French and Israelis devised a plan whereby Israel would launch an attack on the canal and the British and French send in a force to keep the peace. They made landings but received no support from the USA, or Russia and the troops were withdrawn, but many British lives were lost.

Anyway during this fracas which took place between the years of 1951 to 1956, much to my amazement I was recalled on what was known as Z call up. Which resulted in my having to report to an Ack-Ack unit in Norfolk, duration unknown but which turned out to only be two weeks, at a place called Stiffkey on the coast. It turned out to be a Norfolk regiment and the chaps were very friendly. I was able to visit Norwich city and the town of

Swaffam during that time and in fact it made a nice break from routine, but it was nice to get back home to the family

The Car

I had thought for some time that having passed my driving test, it would be nice to have a car, so that we could travel to Staffordshire more often to visit Gwen's mother, and family.

We could only afford a cheap old second hand one of course, but we discussed this together and on the spur of the moment, studied the local paper. There was a garage in a nearby village advertising a car for £25. I knew that I couldn't expect much for that kind of money, but £25 was quite a lot of money to us in those days, but we decided that we could afford it, so we set off to walk to this village intending to drive it back. On arriving there, we had a chat with the proprietor and studied the car. The governor was then called away and left us in the charge of a mechanic, who whispered to me, "Take my tip mate, don't buy that, there is a much better one here for £45 and it is as sound as a bell!" So after some discussion we decided to buy the other one, a sturdy Hillman Minx and parted with our hard earned cash in return for the paper work and keys. Then they said, "By the way, are you insured?" I hadn't thought of that being new to the business of owning a car. "Oh well they said, you hadn't better drive it home then had you?" We explained that we had walked there expecting to drive it back, so they drove us home. I then acquired insurance and collected the car. We were really chuffed as not many working chaps had a car in those days.

There was no MOT, no motorways, traffic lights, roundabouts, yellow lines, one way streets, parking restrictions, traffic wardens, pedestrian crossings, tire tread depth, or any of the petty irritations that we get today, except that one could only park on the near side at night and must show a small light on the off side. Little side lamps were on sale for this purpose and you simply ran a wire from the battery to it.

Spare parts were easily obtainable second-hand and people did their own repairs. We hand painted the car royal blue and christened her Bessie! We used to run up to Staffordshire twice a year 200 miles each way, no bother at all, it took all day, but we enjoyed the journey, except when it rained for we had no windscreen washers, and we had to get out and wash them when splashed by a lorry, but there were not many lorries then, all freight went by rail.

That car was so strongly built that you could drive it into a wall and get away with it. We used to pat her at the end of our trip and say "Good old Bess!" and we meant it. We had her for quite a few years, and I used to do all the maintenance and repairs necessary. Alas when we took up a mortgage to buy our house we couldn't afford to run her and I had to sell her but I wish that I still had her, she would be valuable today as a veteran car, but spares wouldn't be so available and cheap as they were then. It used to be a pleasure motoring up to Stoke taking your time along country roads and enjoying the ride. There is no pleasure in motoring now, everyone is in such a tearing hurry and pushing you on and it is just a case of getting from A to B as fast as possible. I suppose that we were lucky to have been able to potter along in a leisurely fashion. Leaded petrol was the thing then, there was no unleaded.

Our House

As I said, we were looking for a house to buy, that may suit our price range and one day in the course of my work, I had to call at an empty house to take a final reading of the meter. It was a six roomed villa in a country road. The front of the house was covered in large pink roses and I thought how pretty it looked. There was a drive that would take three or four cars and a long garden at the back leading down to fields, with cattle and horses in them.

The property had obviously been neglected over a number of years and needed some renovation, but I could see that it had quite a lot of potential and being a DIY enthusiast, doing it up wasn't beyond my capabilities. Owing to the state of it I thought that we could perhaps get it at a reasonable price. If that was so and we could see our way clear to take it on, we said let's go for it even though we would have to make some sacrifices. Gwen and I saw the estate agent and settled on a price that we could afford, so we negotiated with a building society for a mortgage and paid the deposit. We obtained the key and eagerly started work on the decorating. The very first day that we started stripping the old wallpaper off, we felt itchy and when we got home found that we were lousy with fleas and had to undress in the bath to get rid of the fleas. Gwen was terribly bothered about this and declared that she would never set foot in there again, which of course meant that we would lose our deposit and the house. She went to the estate agents and told them about it and they advised her to go to the council. So Gwen went to the council office and tearfully told them of our plight.

They were very understanding and cheered her up saying that they could fumigate the place and that we would have no more trouble afterwards. She gave them the key and they said now you stay away for three days and we guarantee that you will never be bothered with that again.

The stuff that they used was so strong that the chap next door thought that he had a gas leak and notified the gas board. After that no insect survived in there again even flies died if they came in. The smell soon vanished and we had no more trouble in that direction and moved in. The neighbours told us that the previous occupier was a big "busty" blond woman who was the "village bike" during the war and she hid her husband under the bed all through the war to avoid him being called up. If the place was in that state, he was welcome to it!

They also had the house over run with dogs so no wonder that it was lousy. The gravel drive needed patching in places, so I carried a sack and shovel with me at work so that if I came across any I could pick it up. I nearly came a cropper over this though, as we were forbidden to carry anything except gas board property and one day as I came out of a house, there was a flashy gent waiting for me. He introduced himself as the Gas Boards Auditor and wanted to study my book and cash. I said "Not blooming likely, I don't know you, where's your ID?" He then produced his identity card and said that I was good to challenge him. Being satisfied with the cash and booking, he wanted to inspect the contents of the side box.
"What is this?" he said "This is not board property" but I had my answer to that one, it happened to be in the winter time, and I said "Look I have to travel long distances, and if I get snowed up a long way from home, this is to help me keep going" He said "Oh I see," and off he went and I heard no more about it.

The Accident

I suppose that it is inevitable when riding a motorbike all the time that one is going to have an accident sooner or later. On July 27th 1959, our wedding anniversary, I had arranged to take Gwen out to dinner, but instead ended up in hospital. While pottering along quite steadily up hill on this bright summer morning, the bike suddenly upended and there was I sprawled in the road with the bike on top of me. The back spindle had broken and by chance this had happened right outside of the back entrance to a cottage hospital and the next thing that I knew, two orderlies in white coats doubled out smartly, lifted the bike off of me and deposited me on a stretcher, I protested that I could walk but they wouldn't hear of it. Apparently something had penetrated my left thigh. They carried me in and deposited me on a trolley, while they undressed me to examine the wound. It must have been dodgy for they decided that I needed an immediate operation and gave me a pre-med injection.

I was still semi-conscious as they laid me on the operating table and in my fuddled state I noticed one of the operators in his green robe and mask, go over to a corner and pick up a thick walking stick which he raised above his head handle uppermost and advanced towards me in a menacing manner. I thought Crikey they can't be that primitive; he is going to knock me out with it. I couldn't have dodged for the injection was now taking effect and I couldn't move. I needn't have worried, for when he got to me he reached up with the stick and hooked it in to the big lamp over head to pull it down. At that stage I lost consciousness and the next thing that I knew I was coming round on a bed in the ward.

The Gas Board had notified Gwen and a friend drove her to the hospital. She walked in as I was coming round and I told her about the walking stick incident, that cheered her up a bit, but this wasn't the way that we had planned to celebrate our wedding anniversary by any stretch of the imagination.

This was a small hospital so there were only about a dozen men in our ward, but two of them stand out in my memory. One was an American off of a racing yacht, whose name was Bill White and the other was a little Chinese seaman named Mack Tack. Mack's bed was about halfway down the ward and I noticed that he didn't take part in the general chit chat that went on but just sat there looking lost. I asked the nurse about him and she said that he couldn't speak English and had no pals to visit him, as he was off of a Dutch ship that had since sailed. I felt sorry for him and asked if his bed could be brought up next to mine, as I could use sign language to some extent and would try to cheer him up. I asked if he could have a deck of playing cards as the Chinese invented them and had they contacted the Seaman's mission? It hadn't occurred to them to do this, and after they did so he received some Chinese books from them. I used to watch him reading, as you know when we read our eyes flick from side to side, across the page, but of course reading Chinese characters, his flicked up and down.

Within a little while Mac was like a different person. I used to buy him ice cream as he didn't seem to have any money and he would say "Tank much" which is all that I was able to teach him in English. I looked at his books out of curiosity and according to the pictures they appeared to be quite saucy. He soon perked up now that he had something to do, and in his way he led us to understand that he had a wife and child in China and was anxious to get back to them. He left the hospital before I did and he came over to my bed took hold of my hand and said tank much, but his eyes spoke volumes so that I knew that he had appreciated what I had tried to do on his behalf. Bill White was a very friendly type as most Americans are; he was off of a racing yacht at Cowes, waiting to take part in the Cowes Week races. His mates used to come crowding in regardless of visiting times, or how many were allowed to visit at any one time. They would come stampeding down the ward shouting "Hi Ya Bill!" the whole crew at the same time it seemed. At that time, every time that the radio was switched on, it was always western cowboy music and I said, "You must think that you are back home hearing that stuff all the time," and he said "No we don't go for that there Hill Billy stuff no more, that's what we call 'shit kicker music'. When it came his time to leave the hospital, he came to me with a worried frown on his face and said "Here Hilt,' what am I supposed to do about paying for my treatment?" And I explained about the national health scheme that we have in England, which covered foreigners as well. He was dumb founded and said, "Back home the treatment that I have had here would have cost me hundreds of dollars," so I said "Thank your lucky stars that you had your illness in England then and not in America. No Bill it won't cost you anything, but it would be nice to give the nurses some chocolates or something in appreciation," and that is what he did.

My mate Ken came in to visit me one afternoon, he had brought a coach load of people to Cowes for the fireworks and producing a bottle of beer he announced that he would be able to stay until midnight. I laughed and said, "You won't you know, you will be kicked out when visiting time is over". It was nice to have his company though, as he was such a good mate. By the way I should mention that he was Kay's father and as nice a chap as you could wish to meet.

At long last they let me go home, but my leg wasn't healing as well as expected and I had to attend the local hospital three times a week for treatment and it left me with a nasty scar. If I had been a woman, I could have sued them for a large compensation. They admitted that the accident was caused by metal fatigue causing the spindle to break. I was awarded £75 through the union pressing for damages and when I started back to work again, they wanted to claim the £75 back because they had been paying my wages all the time and I had been off work for four months. I contacted the union and was told to forget it that the matter would be taken care of and I heard no more about it.

So now I was back at work, but thank goodness that is the last I saw of the motorbike, I suppose that I should thank my lucky stars that the accident happened when I was travelling in a town and going slowly up hill. I used to go very fast in open country and if the spindle had broken at speed, I could have been killed. As it is here I am back to the grindstone.

Cut Offs

The most unpleasant aspect of my job was trying to collect unpaid bills, tracing missing debtors and cutting off people who couldn't or wouldn't pay. 'Mere was humour even in these situations as we had to listen to all kinds of excuses some of which were so implausible, that it was often difficult to keep a straight face. In the old private days when most hoteliers and business people were shareholders, the company would allow them to amount quite large debts and pay the bill when the money was available. So that hoteliers would close down at the end of the summer season and go off abroad, not returning until the spring, in time to collect the deposits of bookings for the coming season.

Meanwhile Muggins would be knocking on their door vainly trying to collect the bill and then when they did return, they had the nerve to tell you "Oh I can't afford it now, you will have to wait for the deposits to come in and then I will pay it! Improbable as it may seem now, that situation was accepted, and the bill was paid eventually. The fact that most of them were large shareholders had some bearing on the matter in the old days, but after nationalization this didn't apply, a fact that we had to bring home to them, they had used the gas and must pay up promptly like everyone else, they didn't like it and would muck us about out of spite and we had to listen to what they thought of nationalisation!

I used to do everything in my power to avoid cutting people off, but alas there were times when I had no alternative. It was quite a complicated business in as much as ample warning and every opportunity to pay must be given and there were many rules and regulations that had to be adhered to. When all this has proved fruitless the next step is to attend the County

Court to obtain a warrant of entry, this in itself is quite an experience since one had to enter the witness box and take the oath, state the business in hand and satisfy the magistrate that a warrant is justified, without ever mentioning the customer's name.

Having obtained a warrant, the next step is to arrange a meeting at the address with a policeman, a carpenter and a gas fitter. On previous visits I would have noted the best way of getting in having exhausted all enquires for a key from the neighbours and estate agents. On one occasion we had to gain entry to a house that had sash windows, which normally can easily be opened with a hacksaw blade or a piece of wire. It was raining heavily and the guttering was broken just above the window that I was trying to open, I was working under a miniature waterfall but thought that I would have the window open in a jiffy. Sure enough I slipped the catch in no time, but the sash wouldn't move, it had been nailed down, so wet and bedraggled we tried the front window, once again the catch was slipped quite easily and this time we pushed the catch up but were stymied again it was double glazed and locked from the inside. While we stood there in that rain soaked front garden wondering what to do next, a small school boy walked up the path, pushed open the front door and walked in. We sheepishly looked at each other and burst out laughing. We always tried the door first after that. Our head office had now removed to Southampton from Portsmouth and they were even more strict about bad payers, or 'Cut Offs' as they were termed. I had given every opportunity to one person to pay up and she kept fobbing me off with promises and excuses. I knew that her husband was in regular employment and head office was on my back telling me to cut her off so I made an appointment to do so. This was a job that I could do myself by simply inserting a disk in the inlet pipe of the meter which was in the kitchen.

She invited me in quite nicely and said that she was in the process of cooking her dinner. "Oh that's all right" I said, "I don't mind waiting," and I stood in a corner of the kitchen while she manoeuvred a large frying pan full of bubble and squeak on the gas stove. I should mention that they had previously been using a slot meter, but her son had broken it open twice, or at least he had got the blame, so now they were using a credit meter for the first time, anyway as she stood there she started muttering to herself, quietly at first and it was getting louder, I realized that she was cursing me and the gas board in general, she worked herself up into a frenzy and suddenly swung the frying pan round and threw the contents at me. I neatly side stepped and it splashed all over the wall. I said "Oh Dear! You won't be needing your gas now will you?" And I cut it off and got out as quickly as I could, I imagined her saying to her husband, if you want your dinner it is on the wall!

One house I tried at all times of the day to find them in, as I knew that they lived there, I had left appointment cards which were ignored and I was fed up of getting no reply, so when I called one morning and got no reply, I knocked at a neighbour's door and enquired when was the best time to call. He is in now she replied there is his car. I returned and hammered on the door until I heard footsteps coming down the passage. Suddenly the door was violently flung open to reveal this great big bloke with his fists up. "Clear off" he bellowed, "or I'll knock your block off'!" I about turned and said "Alright chum you have done it now, we will cut you off in the road and you will have to pay to have it re-instated."

I sat in the van writing a report that the customer threatened me with violence and I recommended that we cut him off in the road. I think that perhaps his wife calmed him down, because he came up and apologized saying that he didn't mean it. I said "You may not have meant it Matey, but I did, you have mucked me about for the last time," and I started up the van and left. He must have rushed up to the showroom and paid in full, because the job was cancelled. We had no more bother at that address.

Once I literally had to lead a husband 'up the garden path' it happened like this. I had left a letter on several occasions explaining what would happen if the bill wasn't paid. I called there again and the lady was at home "Oh my God!" she exclaimed "my husband will kill me, he gave me the money but I spent it. Can you call back tomorrow and I will borrow the money from a friend?" The next day she came to the door and whispered that her husband was at home, if I could distract him she would put the money on the seat of my van. With that he came to the door and greeted me I remarked on his beautiful garden and obviously hit on the right note. He invited me to go and see his vegetable patch, so we strolled off up the garden path while his wife sneaked out and put the money on the van seat. Another job done! Some people made no attempt to pay their bill in the usual manner, knowing that eventually I would have to call and collect it, then I would be greeted like one of the family! "Oh come on in gas man, would you like a cup of tea? Been fishing lately?" They would chat about anything at all to avoid parting with their money until the very last minute, I would sit there with my receipt book open and pen poised but they would prattle on stalling for time, this sort of thing was all very well, but very time consuming.

When asked why they didn't pay at the showroom like everyone else, they would make all kinds of excuses not to do so. The favourite one was "Oh the last time that I went in there they were very rude to me and I won't go in there again." I knew that this was most unlikely, but you don't argue when trying to get money out of people.

Obviously some people are lonely and if only you had the time they would tell you their life story twice over. Some old ladies would ask how old I thought they were. This puts you in a delicate situation straight away, so I would give a low estimate, so that they could triumphantly declare that they were much older than that, then you express surprise and declare that she carries her age well and everyone is happy. These trivialities were all part of the game and taken in your stride.

The jobs that I hated most were meter break-ins. These used to happen even in empty houses when it should be obvious that there is no money in them anyway. Apart from the money stolen, there was the damage to the meter, there was the time taken writing out reports, making statements to the police and giving evidence in court. The first time that I had to do that was an eye opener for me. I knew the accused by reputation and that he had a record of petty crime. To listen to his solicitor though, he was as white as the driven snow, the victim of circumstances beyond his control and so on; in fact, it was such a pitiful tale of woe that it was laughable. Looking around the court at all the serious faces, I was amazed that no one saw the funny side of it. His speech was so ludicrous and exaggerated. The magistrate took it all in and gave him a light sentence. That solicitor would have made a good actor, maybe he belonged to the amateur dramatic society, for he certainly knew how to put a sob story across.

One of the magistrates was a chap that I knew well and if he happened to be on the bench when I was giving evidence, he would pull faces at me and ask all kinds of awkward questions on purpose. When we were kids he was the son of the local coal merchant and a staunch member of the Band of Hope that we used to attend and I got to know him well.

Jammed coins were often caused by people inserting all kinds of unlikely things into the meters, like discs made of linoleum, tin, plastic, even cardboard, as well as foreign coins. It is now a criminal offence to try to defraud the company, but we used to turn a blind eye as long as the charge was covered which it often was because the discrepancy would be covered by the rebate due. What I hated was when they used to blame the kiddy. I used to think you rotten coward, fancy blaming the poor little kid!

Full boxes which as the name implies, were meters that had been filled up with coins and needed emptying urgently. These were often caused by the people who should have had a credit meter, but refused to do so preferring to pay as they used the gas. Oddly enough gas was dearer on the slot meter than it was on the credit meter.

One eccentric old lady phoned the head office and declared that no one must touch her meter except Mr. Kemp. So from then on they used to say that my girlfriend needed me, as she was always pestering. They should have seen her she must have been rattling on for 90 and always powdered up so that you would think that she had stuck her head in a bag of baking flour every morning. She got hold of my phone number and would phone on Sundays, holidays or any when and expect me to come to empty her meter. She could afford to have a credit meter but refused to have one. The resident fitter in her village had to make a long detour to avoid passing her house, because if she spotted him she would insist that she had a leak and demand that he attend to it immediately. The poor postman too came in for his share of being pestered and she was the terror of other tradesmen as well.

Account queries were tricky because the complainant would often have used the gas and not realized it. They would say that their meter was either wrongly read, or faulty. They usually knew what their average bill was, but by chatting amiably with the customer, I was often able to establish a reason for the discrepancy. Perhaps they would tell me that they had just had their daughter and her young family staying with them on holiday. They hadn't realized that they had used much more hot water because of this, or cooking and heating. Or it had been an exceptionally long hard winter. Usually the cause was something simple that the customer had overlooked. If a satisfactory solution couldn't be found and the meter had been read correctly, one could sometimes get away with leaving it to see how it worked out the next quarter. If, however the customer was adamant that the meter was faulty, we would have to warn them that if it was sent to the ministry of fuel and power for testing and found to be correct, that there would be a charge for testing it, but no charge if it was faulty and they would receive a refund.

Sudden drops in consumption were treated with suspicion. If there wasn't a satisfactory explanation, either the meter was at fault, or there was a fiddle going on. It may seem inconceivable to you that people would risk blowing up the whole house to save on their gas bill, but it has happened. They either bypassed the meter, or turned it in reverse and reconnected it before the reader called. When we suspected that such a thing was happening, all that we could do was to change the meter and then call frequently to check that all was in order. Now a-days there 's a locking device to prevent that happening.

Secondary meters as used in hotel rooms and boarding houses etc., were always of the slot type and were used to feed the fire and perhaps a boiling ring as well. The gas for the whole premises was registered and paid for through the main meter. The proprietor had full control over what he charged through the secondary meter and the luckless occupier of the room was often over charged. We received bitter complaints but were powerless to do anything about it. There is now a law against overcharging.
Every time that the price of gas went up we had to change all the settings on the slot meters, until they wouldn't go any higher and then they all had to be changed to another mechanism to take the higher settings. When I first started work in 1935 the meters took old pennies and the collectors pushed a hand cart round with the bags of pennies in it. Then they were changed to take a shilling piece. One shilling was worth twelve pennies and the gas value was 186 cubic feet per shilling. Everything had to be altered again when decimalization came in and they were all changed to take the new 10p pieces. This caused some problems because we had to change our way of thinking when counting out the coins. Since decimalization the price has gone up and up, until they took £1 coins.

Along the way we changed to North Sea gas which needed less gas to produce the same heat. I am told that one can now buy an amount of gas at a shop or post office, this is stamped on a card and the card is inserted in the meter.

I haven't mentioned dogs much because they didn't bother me, often people would say how on earth did you get by that dog? It didn't even bark! It is all a matter of approach. Some badly trained dogs would go hysterical when a stranger arrives, it didn't deter me I would advance slowly talking to them and holding out my hand for the dog to sniff and let them know that I was friendly. The most bitten man in our team was petrified of any dog large or small, which bears out the old saying that they can sense your fear and that dogs can tell if you like them or not.

I was once bitten by an Alsatian, but it was my own silly fault. There was a sign on the gate "Beware of the Dog." The gate was open and there was no sign of a dog so I assumed that they had taken it for a walk. I walked up the side passage and I should have whistled or made a noise, for as I turned the corner to the back door the dog was sleeping across the threshold, my sudden appearance startled it and it leapt up and bit my arm. The woman was full of apologies but I reassured her that it was my fault and the dog was in no way to blame and I wouldn't report it. I went and had a tetanus jab just to be on the safe side and I took notice of "Beware of the Dog" signs after that.

Our Dinky

Gwen had a part time job waiting at table in the summer time when we were in the flat and she became friendly with one of her workmates named Sheila. We were visiting at her house one day and she showed us her miniature poodle bitch which was pregnant and asked us if we would like to buy one of the pups when they were born. We were tempted, but uncertain and debated for, and against, until they were born and we went round to see them. They were beautiful little bundles of fluff, we had never seen poodle pups before and they were so pretty, the smallest one seemed to take a fancy to me and I just couldn't resist it. To see one, you would never guess that it was a poodle pup.

So we looked forward eagerly to the day when we could bring it home. We bought a little dog basket and some toys for it, but he was so small that we had to put two books of different thicknesses to make steps for him to get up into his basket. We decided to call him Dinky. He was one of the family and went everywhere with us, even into church once to a wedding and no one was any the wiser. We even took him on holiday once to a flat in Bournemouth for two weeks 'No pets allowed' and got away with it.

Eventually Gwen got a full time job with Sheila in Newport which meant being away all day and leaving Dinky on his own, but I made sure that I called in every day at lunch time to let him out and took him for a walk every evening wet or fine and he soon settled down to the routine and was no trouble at all. We never ceased to marvel at his intelligence, he anticipated our every move and some words we had to spell, as he understood what was said. He would be at the bottom of the stairs if one of us was up there so that he could keep an eye on both of us and not miss anything.

When Barry eventually had a car, Dinky knew the difference between his engine noise and mine. He would be up at the window on the dot that any of us was due home and it was almost as if he could tell the time.

Gwen's Mother was very fond of him and when she fell ill Dinky would lie on her bed with her, but when she died he wouldn't enter the room again. Gwen's brother picked him up and carried him in there once just to see what would be his reaction and he howled pitifully. Also there was an old shed at the bottom of our garden which was there when we bought the place and he wouldn't enter that either under any circumstances. It was as though he sensed something sinister about the shed.

Whenever I tried to mow the lawn, he would drop his ball right in front of the lawnmower so that I had to stop and throw it for him and I used to grumble about it. He used to walk miles with us and when he got tired it was no trouble to pick him up and carry him.

Unfortunately, when he was eleven years old he developed heart trouble and there came a time when we were advised to have him put down. It was one of the hardest decisions that we ever had to make, but we couldn't bear to see him suffer and it had to be done.

I had to screw up all my courage to take Dinky to the Vet for the last time and I felt as though I was betraying my best friend, as indeed he was. He was born on 27-2-1963 and we realised later, that he was put down on the same date 27-2-1974. We brought his body home in a great state of sorrow and I buried him deep in the garden where he used to play, together with all of his toys and I remember thinking that I wouldn't care if they had buried me with him. Anyway I finished the job and covered the spot with daffodil bulbs.

The very next time that I mowed the lawn I imagined that he was jumping round like he used to do and dropping his ball in front of the mower. I felt it so strongly in fact that I came indoors and said to Gwen we will have to move, I hate that garden now, Dinky was with me the whole time that I was mowing and Gwen said "yes I know, I saw him through the window.

Moving

Another reason to consider moving was that they were building a new housing estate all over our lovely view, and they were widening our country lane into a road with pavements and streetlights, thus altering our whole environment. It was time to move on. The council had compensated us for taking some of our frontage and the road was now finished.

We started looking around and as Gwen was now working in Newport we looked in that direction. I was mobile in the firm's van and Barry was working at Cowes, so it made sense.

There was a nice little two-bedroom bungalow for sale in a quiet country lane with lovely views and we fancied it, there was only one snag, it was all electric with oil-fired central heating and no gas in the place, but we went ahead to buy it. After twelve years of occupation we had greatly improved our present home with expensive additions like a bathroom and sun room built at the back. I had put sliding doors in every room and a wash hand basin in the front bedroom. with hot and cold water.

We put the place up for sale and awaited prospective buyers. I am sure that some people get a kick out of viewing houses for sale, for some out of pure nosiness, with no intension of buying, for we had some strange types calling and asking all kinds of questions.

One evening after dark we said "Oh well we won't get anyone else today now". When there came a young couple at the door to view the house, we said "Yes carry on help yourself," and didn't bother to show them round. After all they couldn't see the garden which was our pride and joy, but that didn't seem to bother them and we told each other as they went upstairs that we wouldn't see them again, but to our surprise they came down stairs, and said that they were taken with the place, and could they bring their parents to see it? Of course we said Yes thinking that they would be coming another day, but just as we were thinking of going to bed, the couple turned up again with their parents and again we told them to go ahead and help themselves and take their time. In the end they decided to buy it and then we were able to go ahead with our bungalow, which was called Brambledown .

We had bought that first house for £1,350 in May 1960, it doesn't seem much now, but it was a struggle for us to pay off the mortgage at the time Brambledown was a new experience being all electric. Luckily the previous owner was moving to a hotel that he owned and didn't need his electric cooker, so that we were able to buy that and various other items of furniture off of him quite cheaply.

The removals were carried out quite smoothly and we soon settled down to a new routine, as one does when moving from a house to a bungalow. The price of oil was not exorbitant at that time, (although it became so later) and the heating system worked very well. Eventually though as the price of oil rose higher and ever higher, we had to have the Gas brought in to the premises at great expense and converted to gas central heating.
We were high up on a hill with extensive views of the countryside facing westward, so that we were able to enjoy the beautiful sunsets. The lane was un-adopted by the council so they hadn't gone mad with pavements and street lights. It wasn't a smooth surface but rough gravel which discouraged sightseers cars coming up to admire the view. The bungalows were only built on the upper side of the road with fields on the other side, so that the views of the countryside were unrestricted and stretched for miles.

Barry's Wedding

Barry was married on the 7-9-1974 and had a flat in Sandown. He married Phillipa, a girl whose father was the Verger at Whippingham Church, which Church by the way used to be attended by Queen Victoria and was therefore a tourist attraction.

On his wedding day, it was blowing a terrific gale, but kept dry for the photos and it went off very well. The first week of the honeymoon was spent in Jersey and the second week in Paris. They went across to Southampton on the car ferry owing to the high winds and a workmate of mine picked them up and drove them to the airport. Despite the gale they got away alright but it was a rough crossing and none of us will forget the high winds, on the day.

Sonia & Fred

Gwen became friendly with a girl named Sonia at work, and her husband Fred. We became good friends, and visited each other often. Gwen used to go to bingo with Sonia, while Fred introduced me to the Gurnard Angling Club of which he was a member. They were a fine crowd of chaps so I joined and was soon roped in as treasurer, which I did for twenty years until I had to give it up owing to Gwen's ill health. I remained as a normal member afterwards.

Fred was an organizer and suggested that we should hire a mobile home for our two weeks' summer holidays, taking turns at driving and the four of us to go off together. Our first trip was to Scotland, stopping off at the Lake District on our way. It was marvellous and we had many fine holidays in this way, going to Cornwall, Devon and many other places.

We also had a week boating on the Norfolk Broads in a hired launch and we enjoyed it so much that we did the same thing on the River Thames on another occasion. The scenery was beautiful.

Grandchildren

Phillipa was expecting a happy event, and we all looked forward to the time when our first grandchild would be born. At last the joyful day arrived and Phillipa had a son on the 12-11-1976 a time of great jubilation and excitement. He was christened Daniel Rowland Hyatt Kemp at Whippingham Church, of course!

Barry and Pip moved soon afterwards on 1-2-1977 to 106 Avenue Road, Sandown. We helped them to decorate and on taking up a floorboard were surprised to find grass growing quite thickly underneath.

Two years later we again had the good news that Pip was expecting, it was an anxious time because Daniel had been born by caesarean section, so it was a hospital job, but it was successful and we were delighted to learn that this time it was a girl and Rebecca Jane was born on 22-3-1979. So now we had two grandchildren born two years apart.

Holidays

Brother in law Ray had a caravan in Snowdonia, North Wales and invited us up there for a fortnight's holiday which we gladly accepted. The four of us and the two children travelled up there in our two cars and we had a lovely holiday at Porthmadog in September 1979. Rebecca was only six months old. I shall never forget the journey home, as we had to leave there in the early hours of the morning, so that it was pitch dark and driving round the mountains our headlights were shining straight out into space at times, as we came round the bends. We picnicked at Devils Punchbowl I remember and although it was a bit scary trying to keep up with Barry we arrived home safely.

Fred and I only went astray once on our mobile homes trips, he was navigating and I was driving, we were looking for St Mary's Bay in Devon, anyway we were going down this narrow lane and it seemed to go on for ever, getting narrower all the time, there were no houses and no turn offs, I kept asking Fred if he was sure that we were on the right road and he wasn't sure so we looked out for sign posts but there were none, and eventually we arrived on the (town dump!) which we thought was very appropriate and had a good laugh. It would have been spooky at night so thank goodness that it was daylight.

The four of us spent a happy fortnight in a flat at Brixham, Devon once. It was over a café right on the sea wall. The way that the houses were standing all the way up the hillsides back from the sea reminded us of Ventnor on the Isle of Wight. We used to watch the fishing boats and crabbers coming in and Fred and I went fishing most days but didn't catch anything. We probably were not using the right technique at least that was our excuse, that was a memorable holiday and we had a soft spot for Brixham ever after, it was outstanding among our trips.

We owe a lot to brother in law Ray though regarding holidays, he always invited us to use his caravans whatever site they happened to be on. Once at Ellesmere Salop with Sony and Fred, another time at Blackpool and as mentioned, at Porthmadog. Even after Gwen's mum had passed away we still used to go up to Doreen and Ray and they would take us across to visit Harry and Vera, and take us for trips in their car to various places that we otherwise would never have visited. They were so very good to us expecting us to feel at home which of course we did.

Greengrocery

Ray had a fruit and vegetable wholesale business with a warehouse in a nearby town, and I used to go there with him to try and help out even though I knew nothing about the trade. Of course they handled large quantities and when I first went there, Ray was serving a customer and said "Put an onion on that gentleman's car Hilt please!" and I thought what the devil does he want an onion on his car for? And then it dawned on me that he meant a sack of onions. I soon got used to the jargon though.

Their son Russell joined the firm on leaving school. We used to help Ray and Doreen making decorative wreaths just before Christmas, in his big double garage, and we spent many hours sorting the artificial flowers and wiring them and mossing the wreaths ready for making up. Doreen ran a fruit, vegetable and flower shop and Ray would also make up wreaths, to order, sometimes to a specified shape for customers.

He was in the fruit and veg trade all his life until he sold up, and took a security job with a parcel dispatch firm until retirement. Ray had a soft spot for children and would do anything for them and to his nephews and nieces he was the best uncle that they ever had, in fact I should think that Father Christmas took second place to Uncle Ray.

He would help any child if he thought that they were in need. This I know for a fact although you would never hear of it from him. They were both hard working people and deserved what holidays they could get; the trouble is that Ray couldn't always go, not being able to find someone reliable to stand in for him while he was away.

The Mobile Home

Ray and his mate Roy once hired a big American mobile home while we were staying there and when they went to collect it they phoned us to say that it was unobtainable and they had got us a hearse instead. This set us thinking, and wondering, but they duly turned up with this mobile home as big as a coach, and we loaded up, there was Ray and Dor, her sister Phillis, Roy and his wife Ann and Gwen and I. We set out down the motorway going south. As a mere passenger I naturally thought that they had a route mapped out, but apparently not, which was typical of them, I was looking at the road map as we came down the M5 when they said "Well, where do you want to go?" By this time, we were near to Weston Super Mare so I asked them if they would like to go there. They all agreed and so we went there and parked up for a stroll along the front.

We stayed the night there and travelled on across north Devon to Clovelly. This is a picturesque little town on the coast which has a fascinating narrow cobbled street leading down to the harbour, it is very quaint with little houses on each side with tiny front gardens and a chapel.

On reaching the harbour and looking out to sea there was a shoal of mackerel just off shore and I said to Roy if I had a hand line with feathers on we could reach them, this was only meant to be a remark in passing, but so impulsive is he that the next thing that I knew he had turned up with two hand lines, which he had bought for the purpose, but of course there were no feathers on them and the shoal had moved on by this time anyway. "Never mind" said Roy, "Let's go fishing". "Well what do you suppose we are going to use for bait?" I asked. "Oh said Roy I never thought of that, have you any suggestions?" So as not to disappoint him I showed him how to knock limpets off the rocks to put on the hooks and we threw out, but the others were not prepared for Roy to fish and we had to pack it up and go along with them.

Ray and Roy wanted to go to the races at Newton Abbot, so we set off in that direction and I wouldn't be surprised if that was on the agenda anyway, knowing them. Newton Abbot is an old country town and we strolled round the market looking at all the various country crafts on show. On driving up to the racecourse, there was a steward on duty on the gate and Roy said "Now all you ladies keep out of sight." He got out and said to the steward "Look we have got four decrepit old ladies on the bus, do you think that you could get us a good view as they have never been to a race track before and this is a special treat for them!" I don't know if any money changed hands, but the official was most obliging, saying "Certainly sir follow me with the van," so Ray drove slowly along behind him right up to the winning post and as soon as his back was turned the decrepit old ladies were up the ladder fixed on the back on to the roof cheering on their fancied horses.

This was typical of Roy he had the cheek of the Devil and got away with it. He was a horsey person and had a horse of his own at home for riding. It turned out that the last race was called a seller's race, traditionally the winner is sold at auction on the spot. When Roy heard this he was after bidding for the horse and we wondered how he would get it home, surely not in the caravan with us? "Oh yes he would" said Ann, so we kept our fingers crossed hoping that he wouldn't get it. After some palaver the sale was withdrawn, but that didn't deter our Roy, oh no he ran round pestering all and sundry that he wanted to buy the horse, he had to give up in the end, it was not for sale and that was that.

We travelled about Devon down as far as Brixham and spent some time there watching the fishing boats come and go and admiring the views. All too soon it was time to make our way back after a marvellous week. The van only did 20 miles to the gallon and it must have cost them a fortune in petrol alone, they wouldn't let me pay a penny towards it which was very embarrassing, but that is the way that they treated Gwen and I we were guests and that was the end of it. Gwen used to say you ought to be ashamed letting them pay every time and I was but there was nothing that I could do about it.

We had many a chuckle as Roy was such a comical character. Just as we had settled down to sleep, having said our goodnights all round and everything was quiet Roy would say "Stop it Ann, leave me alone, take your hand away," and we would burst out laughing. This would happen every night just as we were dropping off to sleep. Gwen right from the start was unable to find a spare bra that she had brought and accused me of losing it. So I got my leg pulled about this bra the whole trip, until we were unloading the van on the last day and it was under the sink in a drawer that we didn't use. Doreen and Phil had given a hand in the packing and had put some of our things in the very drawer that we didn't know existed, so I was vindicated and had the lastl laugh after all.

The Fancy Dress Ball

The most memorable invite that we had from Doreen and Ray' though, was just before one New Year's Eve 1979. Come on up they said, we are going to have a party and bring Sony, and Fred with you. They had arranged to have a fancy dress ball at the warehouse, to see the New Year in, in style This must have involved a tremendous amount of work clearing the stock out and cleaning and decorating the big room, installing the bar and so forth. They had hired and paid for fancy dress for all of us. Gwen was Nell Gwyn with a basket of oranges and looked very pretty. Sony' was a crinoline lady, Fred was resplendent in Arab costume, head dress and robes and I was a Goucho in flared trousers, green silk shirt and sombrero. Ray looked the part as John Bull behind the bar and Doreen too had a pretty crinoline dress. The weather was quite mild for the end of December and we drove up in my Citroen car on A category roads enjoying the journey before the motorways were built.

Lots of photographs were taken of us in our costumes both before and after the event. There was a good crowd of guests there, including Roy in a German officer's uniform and Ann in her crinoline dress. Harry came as Miss Piggy, and Vera as Kermit the frog. One chap came as an Oxo cube and couldn't get through the door, and they had to open the double doors to let him in. We had a great time seeing the New Year in and dancing the night away, doing the old langsyne bit at midnight and carrying on until the early hours. What a surprise awaited us when we came out though, it had snowed heavily and we were wading in it up to our knees. We had to drive home the next day and the car was like a snowball, but we cleaned it off and it started first time. I was dreading driving back all that way on snow covered roads, but there was no need to worry the snow ploughs had been busy and had cleared the roads all the way, and we didn't drive on any snow until we reached the Island, that was snow covered, but here we were not so organized as on the mainland and no clearing had been done. When we got home we found that the water pipes were frozen up and we couldn't put the central heating on. We had to take Sony and Fred home anyway so we had some supper with them and came home to bed feeling very tired after the night before and driving all that way. The next morning, we had to go to work and about midday a thaw set in, so I rushed home but I was too late. A joint had blown on a pipe up in the roof and water was cascading down the bedroom wall through the wardrobe, soaking our clothes and carpets. This just about put the damper on things, and took a lot of drying out and clearing up.

I suppose looking back, it was all part of the adventure, but we were not too tickled about it at the time, it sort of takes the gloss off of things when that happens and Gwen wasn't amused either. But we survived and consoled ourselves that there are worst things at sea.

Phillipa Leaves

Barry and Pip moved to No 3 Heath Gardens Lake on 26 -8-1981, from 106 Avenue Rd Sandown. Of course Gwen and I helped all we could with the decorating, fitting curtains, and kitchen cupboards etc., and then sorting out the garden, cutting the over grown grass, moving the shed, and laying out the borders for planting under Pip's directions, she seemed full of plans for the house and garden at the time.

Daniel started school at Grove Rd Sandown a week later and we thought that everything was fine. Until Pip and her mother called on us a few days later, we greeted them with enthusiasm of course and settled down for a chat, but it soon became clear that this was no social visit, when Pip dropped her bomb shell! "I'm sorry Mum" she said "but I am leaving Barry and going to my sister in Crawley and taking the kids with me." Well, we were shocked beyond belief. "Why what has he done?" Gwen immediately asked. "Oh nothing," she replied, "I'm just fed up with being married, and I am going to make a life of my own and settle down in Crawley."

We were dumbfounded and tried to talk her out of it, but her mind was made up and she was determined to go. "Don't worry though Mum" she said, "You will not be deprived of the kids. I promise that you shall have them during the holidays." We just couldn't take it in and when they had gone Gwen said, "Just wait until I see Barry I'll tell him a thing or two, she wouldn't do this without good reason!" But unknown to us, Barry knew nothing about what she intended to do, in fact he was the very last to know. I recalled that she had mentioned that there was plenty of work opportunity in Crawley, as it was fast becoming a commercial town. Barry was managing a snooker hall at the time and had no inclination to leave the Island. Pip's dad, George, was dissatisfied with his job as verger at the church as the wages were poor, but the flat that they were living in belonged to the church and went with the job. I managed to find a house for them to rent in Ryde and he changed jobs and was going to buy the house.

Barry was working long hours and we hadn't seen or heard from him, as far as he knew everything was normal. We were in turmoil not knowing when she was going.

On Saturday morning 7-11-1981 Barry said to Pip "I'm going to Sandown to collect some shoes that have been mended." She replied "Well you had better say goodbye to the kids then because we won't be here when you get back, I'm taking them to Crawley," whereupon Barry borrowed some money and gave it to her to go with, still not understanding that she was going for good and when he did realize what was in her mind he was in a state of shock as we were and unable to take it in. She was going and he was the last to know and wondering how he was going to break the news to us. He had no way of knowing that she had already told us.

When he at last found the courage to call on us, his mother balled him out as soon as he came through the door, but it was obvious that he was broken hearted and not to blame, it was all cut and dried and within a few days her parents went as well. Daniel started school there on 9-11-1981, so it had all been arranged beforehand.

We were all in despair not knowing if she would keep her word about us having the children in the holidays, but we need not have worried on that score, we had them at holiday times as long as they were at school. All that work and enthusiasm at Heath gardens was in vain as she must have been aware even then that she was going, and of course it had to be sold when the divorce settlement was due and Barry went into lodgings in Ventnor.

The Children's Holidays

Gwen and I of course were in our element with the children and did our best to entertain them. Daniel in particular was fond of visiting Carisbrooke Castle and we used to take them there to see the donkey drawing water on the treadmill from the well and ramble round the walls and ramparts. On one occasion the donkey keeper allowed Daniel who was about 7 years old at the time, to lead the donkey from its stable to the well house and that was a thrill for him.

He used to like to listen to the voice of Lord Mountbatten explaining all the history of the castle on the intercom system. They used to like to visit Blackgang Chine where they could play on all the various novelties provided and see the model dinosaurs and a visit to the crooked house was a must, not to be missed.

Unfortunately owing to subsidence large areas of it have slid into the sea over the years and they have had to expand to other territory to keep it going. Robin Hill was another place that they liked to visit, where they could see the goats, rabbits and deer and play on the wooden forts and castles provided for the children. We would sometimes go on country walks to gather a bunch of wild flowers, or just enjoy the scenery. A trip to Sandown to play on the putting green was another favourite.
We shared a beach hut with Sony and Fred and Sony's sister Norma and her husband Peter. at St Helens beach and we used it often in the summer time. There we would go cockling when the tide was out, swimming and boating in a rubber inflatable and trying our hand at fishing when the tide was in. We had a great time at the beach hut, especially when there was a crowd of us there together.

Sony and Fred were very fond of the kids and would arrive every Christmas holiday, not Christmas Day, as they were always with their Mother for that, to watch them unwrap their Christmas presents. I had a movie camera and projector and recorded some of those Christmas mornings on film, so that we were able to look back and relive those very happy days when they were so young, innocent and adorable.

Norma invited us to her daughter's wedding, Rebecca to be a bridesmaid and Daniel a page boy. This was a society wedding, a top hat and tails affair and much attention was given to detail. Rebecca's dress had to be especially made and fitted and Daniel had to have a grey suit for the occasion. They were very smartly turned out and were a credit to us in their behaviour and deportment. We were very proud of them.

Dungeness

We four Gwen, Sony, Fred and I rented a holiday bungalow at Dungeness Kent one year, and the kids had to come too, so we drove to Redhill, Surry where they were living to collect them and brought them back to stay with us in the (Little House on the Prairie) as they called it. We had some great times there, going to Hythe on the narrow gauge railway, round to St Mary's bay to play on the beach and we had a trip to Tenterden and down to Folkestone and Dover. Dungeness is an unusual place, a spit of land formed by the sea throwing up pebbles over the years, with fishing boats pulled up on the beach and fisherman's huts and shacks.
There is a power station in the back ground and two light houses, one of which is not now in use. If it turns foggy one is apt to be startled by the fog horn suddenly blasting forth in your ear. We got to know about Dungeness through the angling club. A group of us used to go there every year for a week's fishing in November, and Fred and I went with them on several occasions. It is a favourite spot for anglers, because the beach slopes so steeply, that there is deep water just a few yards out and codling and whiting can be caught from there when the conditions are favourable, preferably just after a storm.

We used to motor down there, usually two car loads of us and we would pool our expenses and hire a bungalow for the week, it made a nice break and we had some good laughs.

In those days the journey involved travelling right through Brighton along the esplanade and often car would hoot at us and give the thumbs up at the sight of our rods lashed on the roof racks, probably fellow anglers. We all mucked in together and made a holiday of it. Each individual was his own boss and pleased himself, if he didn't want to fish but watch television or read, that was okay with his mates but usually we all fished together. Some of the younger ones would act the goat and play practical jokes on the others, but it was all taken in good spirits and the victim often got his own back to even the score. One chap bought a large fishing umbrella to use as a wind break and the first time that he put it up, before he could anchor it the wind blew it out to sea and we could only stand helplessly watching it floating swiftly away upside down blown along on the wind probably landing up in France. On one occasion the club treasurer was with us and his mother phoned to say that he had received a letter from the premium bonds and should she open it? I should explain that the club held £100 worth of bonds but they had to be in the treasurer's name, and he also had bonds of his own, so it was touch and go if it was the clubs win or his, so he asked her to check the numbers and it turned out that the club had won £5,000 so we had something to celebrate and imagine what we would do with the money This I should mention was the treasurer before me.

We sometimes would go out in a chartered fishing boat and once when fishing on a slack tide, a chap filleted a cod and threw the skeleton over board, we then moved out to another mark and fished until the tide turned again and came back roughly to the spot that we were in before where upon this chap pulled in the same skeleton that he had discarded and the chances of doing that were very small indeed. I had a big fish on and struggled hard to reel it in, it was weaving to and fro and putting up a terrific fight and after a while as it was getting near the boat, the line suddenly parted and I never did know what it was that I nearly caught, so much for the one that got away!

We often fished at night that being the best time by the light of our Tilley lamps, with a shaving mirror stuck at an angle in the pebbles to reflect the light up to our rod tips and some of the lads would fall asleep when things were quiet, so that the tide would go out leaving their tackle high and dry until they woke up sometimes to find that their mate had attached something comical to the end of it.

We used to hire a freezer to keep the fish fresh until we departed for home again. Fred and I decided to go into partnership to buy an 18ft dinghy. As usual we were not very flush for funds and had to do it by degrees.

So first of all we bought a glass fibre hull from a local factory for £81.40 on the 14-5-1973. One of our club members was a foreman boat builder and undertook to build up the hull for us in his back yard. This entailed steaming and bending the timber for the keel and attaching a steel skid, or keel band to it, next the wooden transom on the stern with two cleats attached. This was followed by the wooden stiffener all-round the gunwale with a cleat at the bows, now comes the three thwarts, the big one in the stern, one amid ships and one forward. Especially shaped wooden brackets were made to fix them on called knees. The timber cost us £20 and £10 for the labour.

Okay so now we have a boat, now we need rowlocks, oars, an anchor, chain and rope and last but not least, an outboard engine. All of these things we were able to obtain second hand through members of the club, also an echo sounder.

Some of the chaps worked in a factory that made bilge pumps and so we were able to fit a pump as well, this is a must for pumping out rain water etc. Now we had to provide a mooring place among the other boats, this is done by driving two long metal poles into the mud wider apart than the length of the boat, so that it can be moored fore and aft.

Now we needed a pram dinghy to get out to her when she was afloat Luckily my next door neighbour worked at a fibre glass factory and made us a dinghy for £18, we fitted this with rowlocks and oars and considered ourselves fixed up but it doesn't end there, the inlet where we moored our boats was tidal which means that you cannot get afloat until about two hours before high tide and you have to return one hour before low tide in the winter time, but in the summer the boats can be moored in the bay and to do this we had to make a concrete mooring block with a chain, rope and buoy attached.

We decided to call the boat 'Kushty Bock' which is Romany for good luck Our boat competitions took place on Sundays, weather and tide permitting A date is fixed and then it is all in the hands of the Gods. We would listen to the shipping forecasts the night before and again in the morning, and it may be touch and go regarding the wind because we wouldn't set out if the wind was above Force 4.

If it seemed reasonable Fred and I would load up our gear in the car and drive down to Gurnard to the club and set out with the other boats, but if it was chancy, the lads would await word from the comp' secretary whose decision was final, if he decides that it is too rough the comp' is cancelled and that is that. It is then open to the individual to decide if he wants to take the risk, but they were sensible chaps knowing that a sudden squall could cause havoc, and didn't take chances.

Another hazard was the unwary yachtsman. When at anchor fishing, you cannot move out of the way quickly, and it was not unusual to see a yacht bearing down on a collision course, with no look out, then we had to shout "STARBOARD!" sometimes several times before someone takes notice and then they are likely to hear some salty language about amateur sailors, and look outs in particular.

Unfortunately, all good things come to an end eventually.

After suffering one heart attack and surviving, Fred suffered another one in the night on 17-2-1984, and the Medics after a hard battle were unable to save him. His sudden death was a huge shock to us all and we were very sad to lose such a good and faithful friend, and help mate. I sold the boat to a club member to pay Sony her share. It is still on its mooring, but has been renamed. I could still go out in someone else's boat if I wanted to, and sometimes did. For quite a while after Fred passed away I couldn't enjoy shore fishing, as I had the uncanny feeling that he was with me, and even passed a remark to him through force of habit I suppose, I would say I've got a bite Fred, and then feel foolish because Fred wasn't there, so I never went shore fishing by myself after that. There are not so many fish about now as there used to be, but I don't fish anymore so it doesn't matter to me. I was treasurer of the club for 20 years until my dear wife fell ill, and I had to give it up being unable to attend the meetings, so they made me President, which doesn't incur any duties, except to attend the annual dinner.

As often happens these days' people are reluctant to take on any responsibilities, or attend meetings, content to let the same people do all the work, until they refuse to continue doing so, and interest in the club fell away. We gave up the club premises, as the rent got higher and higher. No one would take on the job of Shore Competition Secretary. So that left only the boat section, and that is the situation today, there is still a club of sorts but only for the boats.

After Fred passed away so suddenly, the family prevailed on me to retire two years early, saying you don't know how long that you have to live, so why not go now while you are healthy and able to enjoy life, after all you have worked for 48 years! I hadn't thought along those lines, being content to carry on until aged 65 and able to pick up the state pension.

It so happened that the firm had one Reader too many and was looking to make one redundant. I put it to them that if they made me redundant, a Collector could fill my position and a Reader could fill the Collectors position, problem solved. Oh no they said we would have to advertise your job, and yours is a special job that would have to be filled by another Inspector. So they wouldn't make me redundant, and I couldn't get out in that manner.

I then had to make enquires about going on a reduced industrial pension until the two years were up and I could go on a full pension. I was told that if I applied to the social services I could go on the dole, so I phoned them and enquired. Oh yes Mr. Kemp said the young lady you have a dependant wife so you would be entitled to £45 per week. We considered in that case we could scrape by, and I decided to retire on 31-5-1984.

The metering Superintendent said that the staff would like to buy me a present, and asked me what I would like? I had a big lawn at Brambledown, and had thought of buying a scurryfier to clear up the leaves, I mentioned this to him and that is what they presented me with. On the retirement day we all gathered in the office, and drank a toast, and took some photographs, and I said farewell all round, and after handing in all my equipment they gave me a lift home.

Now when I reported to the labour exchange, they said that because I was getting a reduced pension my application would have to go before a tribunal, and that they wiuld let you know the verdict. It turned out that they granted me the princely sum of £7 per week. So I collected that until I came on to the state pension.

For me, retirement meant freedom from time schedules, no longer having to keep appointments, and the ability to do the things that I wanted to do together with Gwen, without having to worry about the time. I could never understand why people were presented with a clock as a retirement present as time should no longer be a prime consideration, having lived by the clock all your life.

At our own steady pace we would drive out into the country and go for long walks over the downs or along the cliff paths. There was always something to do in the garden, as the weeds seemed to thrive where sometimes the plants wouldn't! At weekends during the summer we spent many happy hours at the beach hut with Daniel, Rebecca, Sony and Fred. The kids liked to play in a rubber raft on the beach, but in the early stages we always had it on a long rope for safety against the wind and tide.

Often Sony's sister Norma, and her husband Peter would join us on a Sunday, and if the tide was right we would dig some worms for bait in the morning and fish for flounders in the afternoon. When Fred was alive we used to renovate the hut each spring, repairing the roof, and repainting the wooden cladding sides after the ravages of winter.

This job now fell to me and I carried on doing it on my own, with Gwen's help as the hut was worth keeping in good repair and would have soon deteriorated otherwise. Peter was a strong swimmer, and thought nothing of swimming across the harbour to the pub at Bembridge for a pint. Barry was now keeping company with a young lady named Claire, and occasionally they would join us and go crabbing with the kids, to see who could catch the most. The grandchildren took to Claire right away, and were quite at ease in her company as she is very young at heart.

Norma and Peter lived in St Helens on the Island, and Gwen and I would visit them, and give Norma a hand clearing the weeds. Peter always objected saying that he preferred a wild garden, and would have let the weeds grow, but not so Norma, and she always got her way no matter how much he grumbled. They eventually moved to Totland,, at the western end of the Island, and Peter now takes a keen interest in gardening.

We used to watch the yachts coming into Bembridge harbour, under motor power along a dredged channel which meant that when the tide was on the ebb they had to keep within the marker buoys, and this showed up the unwary amateurs, who would go astray, and run aground on the sand banks. They could wade ashore when the tide was low enough, but they had a long wait until they could get off again.

Peter received an excellent offer for the Beach Hut and reluctantly we decided to sell it. So ended another chapter in our lives but the memory lives on.

Barry and Claire

Barry had gone into lodgings in Ventnor where he met Claire, and they eventually found a flat in Sandown and settled down happily together. Claire is much younger than Barry but the age difference doesn't seem to bother them and they are well suited to each other. On the 7-8-1988 they bought their first home together in Standen Avenue, Newport, and worked hard at decorating it, even removing the dividing wall between the dining room and kitchen to make more space. They both had good jobs, and announced that they intended to get married at the Methodist Church in Quay Street at 11 am on 27-8-1994.

Naturally there was much planning and discussion about dresses, flowers etc. it was then that we really noticed that Gwen who would normally have been keen and full of suggestions, seemed a little vague and forgetful. I had noticed this forgetfulness for some time but didn't attach much importance to it. This being an important event however, made us realize that she didn't seem to be her normal self, and it was indeed the start of her illness. Her brother Ray and Doreen came for the wedding and they too noticed a difference in her.

At the Methodist Church, there are steps leading up to the church door from the pavement and the bridesmaids were waiting at the top for the bride to arrive amid much excitement. When the bride's car pulled up and she was alighting, Keiron fell down the steps and cut his eye open so Helen his mother had to leave the ceremony and drive him to hospital to have a stitch put in the cut over his eye. He was very brave about it all and she soon returned to take part in the service.

The Bridesmaids were Claire's sister Helen with her little daughter Leanna, Rebecca, and Victoria, Claire's stepsister. Keiron, Claire's little nephew was a page boy, and the best man was their friend Adrian Chappell and Claire's brother John and Daniel were ushers. The Shanklin Evening Towns Women's Guild choir of which Claire was a member sang throughout the service, and gave a recital while the bride and groom signed the register in the vestry.

It was a lovely day, the bride was absolutely beautiful and radiant, and everything went off splendidly. The reception was at the Riverside Centre, and the choir sang Down by the Riverside as they left the church after the stacks of photographs were taken from all angles. The honeymoon was spent in the south of France, and on their return they presented us with an album full of wedding photos, and a video of the wedding service, which we treasured. There is a very comfortable relationship between them and the grandchildren, and they get along fine. This is great as otherwise things could have been so very different. Claire and Barry also get on with Phillipa, his first wife, and were always made welcome when they called at her house behalf of Daniel and Rebecca. That too is a blessing.

Dementia

Poor Gwen's memory gradually deteriorated, and after some tests, it was found that she was suffering from Dementia a disease of the brain from which at present there is no cure, and it can only get worse. I did my best to help her and make her comfortable. Our love was so strong that I couldn't bear the thought of losing her even to care in a Home. I was determined to keep her at home and care for her. After four years, we had a Carer calling in daily to help with her ablutions and attend to her welfare. Occasionally I had to take her to a Consultant Psychiatrist for him to check up on her. To my mind that was a complete waste of time as there was absolutely nothing that they could do for her, and he knew it. He simply asked her a few simple questions to check her mental state, and that was all.

The Carer would call every morning to take Gwen to the bathroom, while I would hurry down to the village store to get some provisions. She started coming in February 1998, and I received a monthly bill as I had to pay for the service, but I didn't mind that as I considered it was well worth it for the service that we were getting. A Psychiatric nurse used to call about once a month, and I asked her what was the difference between Dementia and Alzheimer's disease? And she said that in our case they were one and the same.

All our friends and relations were very kind and supportive, and visited us to show that they cared. I was grateful to them for that, though eventually Gwen wasn't very aware of what was going on, and so wasn't able to fully appreciate their good intentions. One day in October on my return from the shop, the Carer told me that Gwen had had a seizure, and she thought she may of had a stroke. I helped to carry her to bed and rang the doctor. When he came he soon confirmed that she had suffered a stroke, and that it had affected her left side.

After a while she was able to get up but couldn't walk unaided, and couldn't use her left hand. I continued to help and feed her to the best of my ability. Eventually Gwen became completely bed ridden, and was unable to walk, or talk and it transpired that she must have suffered another stroke in the night when I was asleep from which she didn't recover.

Now the district nurse was calling in daily, and on Armistice Day 1998 in the morning she said to me "Stay with her I don't think that she will last much longer". I was shocked to hear this, and hoped and prayed that she was wrong, but I did as she said. I stayed with her praying and holding her hand and talking to her, trying to encourage her though I don't know if she could hear me. She was breathing heavily all the while until six o'clock in the evening when her breathing became quieter, and suddenly stopped altogether, and my sweetheart was gone.

I was stunned and ran next door to Alva my neighbour an ex-nurse, who came back with me and took over. She phoned the Doctor and I phoned Barry who was in Southampton on business, and he came as soon as he could. Meanwhile to take my mind off of things while we waited Alva asked me if I had any books on the Isle of Wight as she wanted to show them at her club, and we were looking at these when Barry arrived so that he was surprised to find us doing that instead of in turmoil as I probably would have been if it wasn't for her, thus easing the traumatic moments to follow.

I tried to carry on as normal, but I cannot adequately describe the terrible pain and ache in my heart. People flippantly talk about a broken heart, but it isn't until one really experiences it that you realize the true meaning of the expression. I kept telling myself that it was for the best, a happy release and so on, but I wasn't convinced, and wished that she was still with me. Selfishness on my part I suppose, but it is a true saying that while there is life there is hope, and one clings desperately to that hope.

Now so many little things remind me of her. A familiar tune or joke that we shared, or the progress of the grandchildren that she loved so dearly fills me with sadness, and that awful sadness returns. Everyone has rallied round and tried to help me and I am very grateful to them for that. I can never repay Claire and Barry for taking the load of correspondence and arrangements off of my shoulders, arranging the funeral and dealing with the documentation of insurance, and the Undertaker etc.

My sister Myra, and Gwen's brothers Harry and Ray' came of course. I felt so sorry for Ray, as he and Doreen had just suffered the loss of their beloved granddaughter Leslie, who had died suddenly of a heart attack a short while before, and he was very much in mourning for her at that time. It had come as a terrific blow to them, and he had not yet had time to recover from it and was still in shock. Harry had also lost his wife a few years back, and wasn't in the best of health. As he was a lay preacher we asked him if he would like to conduct the service. It is I know what Gwen would have wanted . He agreed willingly and said that he would be honoured to do it. It must have taken a huge effort on his part, as he was elderly and unwell. Gwen is with me always in spirit, and I constantly think of those true lines, {Do not stand at my grave and cry, I am not there, I did not die}. She will survive in the memory of all who knew her, because she was so well liked and respected. Armistice Day was always a sad time for us as her brother Leslie was killed fighting in Italy, but now, as she died on that day, it is especially significant, and the two minutes' silence has a double meaning for me. The funeral date fell on her birthday the 18th of November. We debated whether to put it off, but decided that it would be appropriate to remember her on that date also. I feel that she is with me and always will as long as I live, as she was the love of my life, and no one or nothing will ever replace her.

Now of course I carried on alone, making the most of my life, and trying to keep up the standards that Gwen would have expected of me, always keeping true to her memory, and in my mind I speak to her all the time, just as I always did, for we included each other in everything that we did, and every decision that we made.

On second thoughts, I am not alone by any means as Claire and Barry were keeping an eye on me, and doing all that they could for me and I was very grateful to them.

Holidays Abroad

They took my sister Myra and I, to France as they had a holiday house in the Dordogne, and we drove over the mountains into Spain. That was a great adventure for us. Myra too has been including me in her holidays abroad. Myra with her daughter Frances, and Frances's husband John invited me to join them on a week's holiday in Tenerife, and I went up to Birmingham to join them. We flew from Birmingham airport on 12-2-1999 they let me have a window seat and I was able to look down on the mountains while flying over the length of Portugal. The accommodation was good, and we thoroughly enjoyed our week there. Spending our days on the beach, and having lovely meals out each evening. The week soon passed as they do when on holiday, but the rigmarole of going through the procedures at the airport were all new to me, and part of the adventure.

They have subsequently taken me with them on other trips abroad, twice to Spain and twice to Rhodes one of the Greek Islands, where I joined them in swimming and snorkelling.

My next door neighbours, Alva and Hector invited me to join their club of pensioners which I did. We meet every Wednesday morning at ten o'clock at the Wootton Community Centre. After the business is finished, we have a beverage of our choice, and usually a speaker is engaged to give us a talk, sometimes illustrated with slides, until 12 o'clock. Members bring things to sell, like surplus garden produce, flowers, fruit, and books, proceeds to the club funds.

In the summer instead of meeting inside, we meet at pre-arranged different venues in the country, and go for a ramble, followed by a picnic lunch, and then usually tea at a member's house. I keep busy in the garden as well, so you see I have plenty to keep me occupied. My sister Myra, her daughter Frances, and Frances's husband John, invited me to accompany them on their holiday at Lindos on the island of Rhodes, having all been arranged by John on his computer through the Internet, a hire car and self-catering for 2 weeks, flying out from Birmingham international airport, on 27/ 09/ 2000.
  I of course jumped at the chance and looked forward eagerly to the trip, and after drawing my Drachmas from the bank, all I had to do was book my ticket on the national express coach to Birmingham and pack my bag with summer clothes. I travelled up to Myra's home 2 days before departure date and we all set off together by taxi for the airport on the 27th.

We boarded on time, but were half an hour late taking off. It should be a 6-hour flight but we encountered some turbulence which set us back a little. Greek time is 2 hours ahead of meridian, so we set our watches. We landed a little later than expected and while John went off to find the hire car, we waited for the luggage to arrive on the carousel and wheeled it off to the car pound. The car was a Renault 2 door hatch back Clio and by dint of skilful packing we managed to cram our stuff in besides ourselves. Frances drove while John navigated and once on the right road she drove skilfully down to Lindos, arriving about 3am far too late to collect the key to the apartment, so there was nothing for it but to sleep as best we could in the car.

It was a warm night and Frances and John decided to go swimming, but not being able to find their costumes in the pile of luggage went skinny dipping. Apart from a little discomfort the night soon passed and about

8-30am we proceeded to a café, while John went for the key. It turned out that the streets were mere passageways no wider than 2 metres and therefore we were unable to park close to the digs and had to carry all our kit, so you can imagine our relief on finally getting settled in our apartment. The landlady greeted us with a sprig of basil which apparently is a quaint old custom. To enter we passed through a pair of large wooden doors into a square courtyard the floor of which was covered in small white pebbles about the size of almonds with a round design in the middle made of black pebbles and a floral margin of black pebbles round the edges. These were fixed and set into the floor and was a common type of patio flooring.

Along one side stood a 2-bedroom unit, then the kitchen and another 2-bedroom unit. Our 2-bedroom unit was across the end of the square, down the other side was the laundry room with a toilet and then the bathroom with shower, bath, bidet, toilet and wash hand basin. There was a notice requesting that toilet paper should be put in the bin provided and not down the toilet owing to the inadequate plumbing and this applied everywhere throughout Greece. The other side of the square was a low wall which gave a view out across the natural harbour.

We were about a half a mile up from the beach and sea, so had a nice view. What meals we had there were taken outside in the courtyard which was shaded by a roof of rush matting. We had our main meals out in the evenings, doing a tour of the restaurants. The very first morning I bought a snorkel and mask and joined in with Frances and John, taking it easy at first until I got used to the idea. The water was warm as clear as glass, and very buoyant, the fish were plentiful, and in fact came right up to the shore so that people were feeding them from the beach with bread.

We swam every day, but Myra was not very keen, and was contented to sit on the beach, and watch the bathers. Lindos was a small town of white-washed houses at the foot of a high hill on the top of which was a very ancient temple come fort called the Acropolis once occupied by the Knights of Saint John and many other invaders in their turn. People come in coaches, and by sea from other islands to see the Acropolis, but the only way to get up there is on foot, or donkey. We used to feel sorry for those donkeys, as they had to carry some very heavy people. We of course walked up, but those donkeys were the only transport, and were called (taxis) a cleaner followed them along with a scoop and brush, there was no training needed for that job, you pick it up as you go along!

There was a petrol strike on the first week that we were there but we were not affected as we had a full tank to start with so we drove about the island visiting other bays and studying the flora and fauna, there were deer but we didn't see any, only goats, 2 cows, no horses, but there are feral cats. The trees are mostly pine, palms, holm oak, spruce, cedar, laurel, olives, pomegranate, fig lemon, and orange. There were lots of prickly pear, grapes, hibiscus, oleander, thorn apple, periwinkle, bougainvillaea, jacaranda, white lilies, yellow poppies, large crocus and cyclamen.

The landscapes were wild and rugged. The mountain roads were very rough, but the other roads were very good, but Greek drivers were quite reckless. There were motorcycles for hire, crash helmets not compulsory. We explored some of the dried up river beds and the pebbles were multi coloured and pretty. There were patches of elephant grass and bull rushes, but we didn't see much in the way of cultivation, it may have been the wrong time of year. There were some pretty villas dotted about along the way with clever wrought iron work gates and arches covered in brilliant climbing plants like morning glory, bougainvillea, and jacaranda making a splash of colour in the sunlight. We enjoyed that holiday very much, but all good things must come to an end and we had to make our way back to the airfield.

We didn't take off until very late, in fact not until 1-40 in the morning, so we enjoyed our last day, travelling back late evening. The flight back was a sleepy affair, but the pilot announced that we were passing over Paris and on looking out of the window, there were the lights of Paris clear to see. We landed back in Birmingham airport just after 4 am and got a taxi back home to Myra's house.

This is only one of many holidays that I have enjoyed with them, having gone to Spain several times and once to Tenerife in the Canary Isles. Myra belonged to a club that goes off on coach trips to different places for a week or two weeks stay and I went along too. Sometimes these trips were in the form of Tinsel and Turkey do's, which I admit I had never heard of until I was invited along. For the benefit of the uninitiated, these trips take place just before Christmas, and the idea is that one enjoys a Christmas in advance at the hotel with all the trimmings and entertainments usually associated with Christmas. I have attended many of these in different venues in both England and Wales. I am also privileged to spend Christmas with Myra's family on occasions.

This went on for several years. I always found plenty to keep me occupied in the garden and then started taking computer lessons once a week. So you see I had plenty to keep me busy and I counted it a privilege to still be able to drive at the age of 93. Also I had been attending computer lessons for about three years and the tutor said that I was ready to take a City and Guilds examination for literary skills. I laughed at that as I couldn't imagine myself passing a City and Guilds exam but I did a trial run and passed that without too much trouble, so I thought that it would be nice if I could pass the actual exam so I entered and to my amazement, I passed.

Daniel's Wedding

We were aware that Daniel was courting a young lady named Amanda and we had met her several times. So we weren't surprised to learn eventually, that they had become engaged.

By coincidence, Myra also received news that her son Clive, who was working as a highways surveyor in Romania, had also got engaged to a Romanian girl named Auralia, or Aura' for short, at about the same time, this they announced when they came to England for Christmas 2002. I am telling you this because it led to another even bigger coincidence. Time passed and then Daniel announced that he and Amanda were getting married on the 23rd August 2003. Then Clive announced that he and Aura' were getting married on very same date in Romania. So I received an invitation to both. They didn't know each other and have never met.

Where I would have been going to both, I had to choose to attend at my grandsons wedding, of course, at Canterbury in Kent. On Friday 21st August 2003, Barry and Claire, Claires mother Hilary and I, motored off to Canterbury. Claire was going to fly to Canada after the wedding, to work out there for a while for her firm, so we had luggage with us. Therefore, Barry had borrowed his mate's Mercedes estate it being a bigger car and left his own car with his mate Tony.

So off we went in style and had a nice smooth ride, until we got to just a few miles from our destination and the overheating light came on. Barry pulled off into the first lay-by that we came to behind a parked lorry, and we looked under the bonnet to find that the fan belt had broken! Well we discussed the matter and agreed that there was no way that we could repair it.

The car's owner, Tony, was in the AA, so Barry phoned them using Tony's name. As a security check they asked for his date of birth and of course Barry didn't know it, so he said that he would get back to them and phoned Tony for inspiration. He gave his date of birth and Barry again phoned the AA with that information and they said that they would come out to us. There was nothing to do then but wait. After a while we were surprised to see a Mercedes breakdown van drive into the lay-by, it turned out that the lorry in front of us was a Mercedes and was waiting on the van coming to repair it.

We couldn't believe our luck. The repair mechanic said, "No problem, I'll fix the lorry first and then do yours." "No" said the lorry driver, "Fix theirs first, I'm on overtime!" So he replaced the belt free of charge and then dropped a bombshell. He said, "I've got bad news for you your cylinder-head gasket has blown!" We explained that we had to get back to the Island and he said that if we drove at a moderate speed and kept it topped up with water, we should be able to continue, but before we left the AA arrived and inspected the engine confirming what the mechanic had told us, so we continued cautiously on our way, having phoned Tony to tell him the news. There wasn't room for all of us in Daniel's house so he had arranged for us to stay at a bed and breakfast place across the road from him. The next morning, we were surprised to see Tony arrive having left the Island early to drive up in Barry's car and arrange for the AA to bring his Mercedes back to the Island on a flat- bed truck. This they did, taking it all the way with Tony as well, across on the ferry to a garage of Tony's choice to be repaired.

We then of course had Barry's car to carry on with, but not so much luggage having left the wedding presents at Daniels House. They were blessed with a fine day and a lovely church wedding with a big reception and lots of photos, feasting and dancing and a good time was had by all. We had to travel back the next day to take Clare to Heathrow Airport. We were feeling guilty about Tony's car as we knew that it would be an expensive job to repair it. In the event it turned out that we needn't have worried. Both the AA and the mechanic were wrong in their diagnosis, as the repair garage reported that there was nothing wrong with the engine so that was a relief all round, but had made Daniel's wedding all that more memorable for that little adventure. Now more great news! I'm to be a great grandfather!

On the 18th September 2004, Amanda gave birth to a healthy baby girl (Imogen Rebecca) and of course this necessitated another trip to Canterbury, to welcome her into the family and more photographs of each of us holding the baby.

Hospital

For a long time, I had a little mole like place on my face, by my right ear. I suspected that it may be skin cancer. I mentioned it to the doctor, because it wouldn't heal up. The doctor arranged a visit to the local hospital for a check-up. Later I had an appointment to go and have it cut out. This was done under a local anaesthetic and involved quite a lot of stitches. I had to attend again in a week's time and have the stitches removed. In the meantime, I saw Barry and Claire off on the ferry for a two week trip to the Red Sea, for a diving holiday. I promised to water their plants and clear their outside mail box every day.

The summer weather was perfect and I was able to do some gardening. Two days later I was sieving some compost in the greenhouse, when I began to feel ill. I was experiencing an ache in my arms and chest which was bad enough for me to have to go into the house and sit down. I used a puffer that I had for my angina but it didn't help. I picked up the phone, intending to ring for an ambulance, but I knew that I had to attend the hospital the next day so I didn't ring hoping that I would soon feel better, which I did after about three hours. I went along to my club the next morning, not feeling too bad and went for my hospital appointment in the afternoon.

When my turn came to see the doctor they greeted me, asked me how I was and commenced to remove the stitches in my face. This was my cue to tell them about the scare that I had experienced the day before. On hearing my story, they were very concerned, saying that I had had a coronary and should have called the ambulance straight away. Having removed the stitches and put on a dressing, I was told not to stand and a wheelchair was sent for. I was lifted into the wheelchair and taken down to the reception ward, where I was put into a bedside chair. I asked if this meant that I was being kept in, but couldn't get a straight answer.

I sat there wondering about my car, which was parked in the hospitals pay and display car park. I asked about this and as told that if I gave them the registration number and told them where it was parked they would attend to it. The next thing on my mind was that I ought to notify someone of my predicament, but how? I had been told that I wasn't allowed to walk anywhere so how was I to get to a phone? There were three of us in the ward, so I chatted to the others and asked about phoning someone.

The chap in the next bed explained that the gadgets over the beds were phones, televisions and radios all in one. In order to be able to use it, you needed to obtain a £5 card from a machine outside of the ward, insert the card into the machine and be signed up to that particular machine. This was no good to me as I had no idea as to how long I would be there.

The chap in the next bed, who had told me about the £5 card, invited me to use his phone. I had two priorities, firstly to notify my next door neighbour of my predicament, a wise move for being a member of the same club, word soon got around, he knew that I had club cash in the boot of my car and arranged for another club member to retrieve it and drive it home for me. The second priority was Barry's mail collection and watering, so I phoned his office and spoke to his colleague, who undertook to do the job. The time now was about 3pm and I sat there for what seem like hours, until a nurse came dashing by. I enquired where the toilet was and if there were any magazines available? She said that I mustn't walk and that she would fetch me a bottle. She then disappeared, never to return so I wandered around until I found the toilet myself.

I sat there for hours, supper came and went and I eventually went to bed. At intervals during the night, we were subjected to long hooting noises and I wondered what they were. In the morning I asked a nurse what it was and she told me that it was the bedside alarms. I wondered why, if they were alarms, that they had to on for so long before anyone answered them. I soon learned of course that there aren't many staff on at night and that everyone had to take their turn. This made me grateful that at least I was not totally bedridden and didn't have to use the alarm to use the toilet, in fact I never did use the alarm button.

During the morning I was subjected to several types of tests, given pills and injections and taken off, by wheelchair, for an X-ray. I was then transferred to a ward with six beds, five of which were occupied by bedridden patients. Up until then I had been wearing one of those back to front hospital gowns which was supposed to fasten at the back, but never do. It was embarrassing to wear so I asked one of the staff that was changing bedding, for a pair of pyjamas. She supplied me with a white jacket and pink trousers that were too narrow at the waist but beggars can't be choosers!

I said a member of staff because it was difficult to know who was who. The nurses wore a blue uniform but were very scarce, whilst others wore a green tunic and presumably were auxiliaries, they were very caring. One old gent had suffered injuries to his face after a bad fall and unfortunately he was unable to feed himself. Communication with him was difficult because he was profoundly deaf and had very poor eyesight. The elderly gentleman in the bed opposite to me had a visit from two scruffily dressed people, a man and a woman, the man had a straggly ponytail and when the patient spoke to him would always reply "Yea, yea, yea" in a loud voice. After they had left the patient had another visitor, this time a woman on her own. She asked if old yea, yea, yea had been in. I couldn't help chuckling so she grinned across to me and said "Well you know what's under a ponytail, don't you?" She was kind enough to get me a card for the TV and phone and showed me how to get signed up to use it.

Shortly after this I was told that my niece was on the ward telephone enquiring about me. I was able to speak to her "Hello Francis, how the devil are you?" she replied that I had better ask my sister that and put Myra onto the phone. Apparently they had been trying to contact me at home and consistently getting no reply had notified the Police. The Police had traced me to the hospital so I had to assure Myra that I was alright.

My next door neighbours, Hector and Alva, visited me in the afternoon bearing gifts, bless them. I had various tests, pills and injections in my stomach twice daily. The food was good; a menu was issued twice a day on which you could tick off your choice from a wide selection. Hector and Alva visited daily and some of the other Club members and a colleague of Barry's looked in from time to time. I wasn't forgotten and felt honoured to receive so much attention. I didn't realize that I was so popular Such is the advantage of being a member of a caring Club and having friends.
My face wasn't healing properly and had to be dressed, but I was in the right place for that. At Doctor's rounds on Friday morning, he said that he would arrange for me to go onto a treadmill for assessment. On Monday he changed his mind and saying that I should do the treadmill at a later date, I could be discharged, after having my face dressed, the following morning. I phoned Hector with the news and he said that he would come and collect me when I was ready.

The next morning Tuesday, six days after being admitted, I was up, washed and dressed and ready to go. I needn't have rushed because I still had to wait to get my face treated and was finally ready to leave at 10.30am. I rang Hector and arranged to wait just inside the entrance doors. I was issued with my pills and some face dressings and arrangements were made for a District Nurse to call to dress it. Hector arrived in double quick time and took me home.

Myra, despite having a broken arm, insisted on travelling down from Birmingham and she arrived the next day. So I am on tablets, probably for the rest of my life, and I have to take a blood test every six months. I felt alright and was able to carry on with my style of living, keeping away from wine, women and song. I just poked about in the garden and joined my friends at the Club for walks and picnics during the summer. Not taxing myself and getting plenty of rest.

Life Goes On

Daniel and Amanda moved from Canterbury back to Redhill, where Daniel had secured a post as Head of Drama at a local school. My second great grandchild Adam was born on the 2nd January 2006. Adam was born three weeks early so Barry was surprised to receive a phone call, announcing the birth whilst he and Claire were travelling in New Zealand. When they returned to England they went straight to visit their new grandson, before returning to the Island. Two weeks later Daniel, Amanda, Imogen and Adam came across to the Island so that I could meet the new baby.

One year later and more good news Amanda was pregnant again, Grace was born on the 08/06/07. Once again we all went up to Redhill to welcome Grace into the fold. Nancy was the next born on 21/12/08 and we thought Daniels family was complete. How wrong we were, to our delight Reuben joined us on 02/03/10.

Over the years several of the Club members became too ill to attend and one by one I attended their funerals. Hectors wife Alva died and the membership was now so small that the decision was taken to disband the Club. I seemed to be forever at a funeral as all of my friends were dying off. Then granddaughter Rebecca and her partner Gavin announced that they were expecting and Rebecca gave birth to Oliver on 03/10/14 Rebecca and Gavin married in August 2015 and naturally Barry, Claire and I attended. It's lovely to have all of the grandchildren and great grandchildren together. One day when I was aged 95 Hector, who was just one year older than me, drove himself to the supermarket and whilst there had a heart attack and unfortunately died on the spot. Barry and I discussed what could have happened if his heart attack had happened whilst he was driving, he could have caused an accident killing many others. I took the decision right then to give up my car and gave it to Barry's wife Claire, I had been lucky not to have been involved with a motoring accident for 50 odd years.

Unfortunately, Daniel and Amanda split up and eventually divorced. The children stayed with their Mother and spend alternate weekends with Daniel, which actually meant that they come to the Island more often and we were able to see more of them. Then Gavin and Rebecca announced that she was pregnant again and my seventh great grandchild, Jessica was born on 20th November 2017. Daniel remarried to a lovely Australian lady Yvette in 2019 and we were once again crossing the Solent to attend the wedding.

It's strange to think that now at the ripe old age of 98 I have known six generations of the Kemp family. They are my grandfather Tom, my father Roland, myself, my son Barry, my grandchildren Daniel and Rebecca, Daniels children: Imogen, Adam, Grace, Nancy and Reuben and Rebecca's children Oliver and Jessica.

I have had a long and happy life and consider myself to be very lucky to have reached 98 and still be reasonably able to manage on my own. My legs started to swell and I had a fall in the summer of 2019, unfortunately Barry and Claire were away on holiday, but my friend and neighbour Alan phoned the doctor. The doctor examined me and thought that I should go into respite care for a few weeks, until I was back to my normal self.
Barry was ringing me daily from Croatia and when he heard about the doctors recommendation asked how I felt about being looked after for a while. I said that I didn't think that it was necessary and would be expensive. He threatened to cut short his holiday and come back to look after me. That is the last thing that I wanted, so reluctantly agreed to go. Barry said "good because I have already reserved you a room at Woodside Hall Nursing Home, for four weeks". He then rang Alan who kindly gave me a lift to the Home.

I had visited the Home before, with Barry and Claire, because Claire's mother Hilary is a resident there. I therefore knew that it was like a 5 star hotel with nurses. They were of course expecting me and showed me to my room. I had a lovely room to myself and the nurses started treating my swollen legs and bruises, from the fall, immediately. All of the time that I was there I was encouraged to do nothing but rest with my feet up.

One amusing incident happened. One day there was a knock on my door and Hilary came in, she didn't know that I was in the Home and had gone with a friend to my house to visit me. Her friend Julie had taken her out for the day in her car and they had decided to come for a cup of tea with me at my home. Alan saw them and explained that I was temporarily resident at Woodside Hall, so they came back to where they had started from.

The food was amazing and after three weeks I asked if I could extend my stay from four to five weeks and then after the fourth week extended to six weeks. I was tempted to stay on but it was so expensive and I would have soon run out of money. Barry collected me after the sixth week and took me back to my own home. It was nice to be back but I have to admit that it did do me good, being looked after so well.

Barry arranged a care package for me, so that I could take things a little easier and now I have carers visit me three times a day. Morning to make sure that I shower, get a breakfast and take my medication, lunch time to prepare me a cooked meal and early evening to make sure that I get a tea. I need to keep going for myself so when the morning carer comes I am already up and dressed, had my breakfast and medication. During the morning I prepare the potatoes and vegetables ready for my lunch, after spending time on facebook.

All the carer needs to do is cook a ready meal to go with them. I tend to put my feet up in the afternoons, doctors orders, so when the third carer comes they get me some tea. I don't feel that I really need them but it is nice to have someone to chat to and takes the pressure off of Barry a little although thankfully he still visits me most days.

I feel now that I have shared everything with you dear reader and I hope that you have enjoyed reading my ramblings. I have to stop writing now and finish this story before its natural end.

It's been a good life "Along the Way."

Along The Way

I learned the way at mother's knee.
"The straight and narrow son," said she.
"You'll find the way is hard and long
but there will be joys as you go along
some happiness will come your way,
troubles come and go, they will not stay."
My pleasures came from homemade toys
and we started work when just mere boys.
But we were free to enjoy the countryside,
or on the sands by the surging tide.
We could play safely in the streets
With no pocket money to buy sweets.
When in our teens there came the war
And allegiance to the King I swore
How young we were without a care,
so innocent, willing and unaware
of what lay ahead just round the bend,
or what we would endure before the end.
When I met my sweetheart one fine day.
I knew that love was here to stay.
Then I was posted to the Far East,
Nearly four years away until the peace
Was signed and I'm home for good
to house hunting, marriage and fatherhood.
Then in later years what could be better
Than two grand-children, Daniel and Rebecca?
It's amazing how the years have flown,
My dear wife passed away and I'm alone
I've no regrets because you see,
Along the way, life was good to me.

By Hilton Kemp

Fever Song

And did you serve in India, lad.
Or Burma's wild green land?
And did you have the fever there
Till you could hardly stand?
And does the fever catch you still
When England's winds blow bitter chill?
And does your head throb once again
As it did then, my lad?
And do you feel the dulling pain
The same as you once had?
And do you, soldier, curse the day
When under those hot skies you lay?
And do you shake and shiver, lad,
And ache to lay you down,
As you did then, short years ago,
Under the jungle's crown?
And do you sigh for water now,
And drink the salt sweat from your brow?
And do your limbs feel far away
In ague's sudden grip?
And do you like the price you pay?
The fever-cup you sip.
For being young in England's Isle
When Hitler saw his war-god smile?
Or do you think of well-known friends.
Men of your company.
Who uncomplaining, met their ends.
Nor looked for sympathy;
But under Asia's brassy skies
Died with this England in their eyes
Their rotted bones in jungle lie
Six thousand miles away —
Lad, what's a fever? You won't die.
You'll live another day —
But God forgive, if you forget
They paid in agony, our debt.
We met, we married a long time ago.
We worked for long hours, when wages were low,

No TV, no wireless, no bath, times were hard,
Just a well at the back and a loo down the yard.
No holidays abroad, no carpets on floors.
But we had coal fires, didn't lock doors,
Children arrived, no pills in those days
And they were brought up, without any state aid.
They were safe to go out and play in the park
And our old folk were safe, going out after dark.
No Valium, no drugs, no LSD,
We cured our ills with a good cup of tea.
No vandals, no robbers, there was nothing to rob,
We felt well off with a couple of bob.
People were happier in those far off days,
Kinder and caring in so many ways.
Milkmen and paperboys would whistle and sing,
And most folks grateful for a very small thing.
We all got our share of trouble and strife,
We just had to face it, 'twas the pattern of life.
Now I am alone, I look back through the years,
I don't think of the bad times, the trouble and tears.
I remember the blessings, our home and our love
And we shared them together, I thank God above.

An original poem written by ex-QAIMNS Nurse Kitty Jones

Holding Carbon Rod from Searchlight (2018)

Making a "Thank You" speech at my 95th Birthday Celebrations.

Hilton Kemp 19.04.21 - 10.02.20

Lightning Source UK Ltd.
Milton Keynes UK
UKHW011416290620
365747UK00021B/551